T0209077

Common Sense
TO THE N^{TH} DEGREE

a no-holds barred analysis of freedom, equality, social issues, education, the work place, and discrimination in america today

ROGER SHUMAN

authorHOUSE®

AuthorHouse™
1663 Liberty Drive
Bloomington, IN 47403
www.authorhouse.com
Phone: 833-262-8899

© 2023 Roger Shuman. All rights reserved.

No part of this book may be reproduced, stored in a retrieval system, or transmitted by any means without the written permission of the author.

Published by AuthorHouse 12/29/2022

ISBN: 978-1-6655-7847-9 (sc)
ISBN: 978-1-6655-7858-5 (e)

Print information available on the last page.

Any people depicted in stock imagery provided by Getty Images are models, and such images are being used for illustrative purposes only.
Certain stock imagery © Getty Images.

This book is printed on acid-free paper.

Because of the dynamic nature of the Internet, any web addresses or links contained in this book may have changed since publication and may no longer be valid. The views expressed in this work are solely those of the author and do not necessarily reflect the views of the publisher, and the publisher hereby disclaims any responsibility for them.

Table of Contents

Acknowledgments

I have a number of people to thank for their encouragement, input, and support. I would like to thank my oldest daughter, Liz, her husband Nathan, and their daughters Alyson and Kaylee. I would also like to thank my youngest daughter Carla and her husband Clayton. I'm sure that I have shirked many family obligations and avoided involvement in a substantial number of family activities in order to afford myself the necessary time to write this book. I have a bunch of chores to make up to even things out. I would also like to thank the mother of my daughters, Carrie, for keeping me afloat on many occasions when I was set to crash and burn.

I would also like to thank my parents, Don and Virginia, for standing behind me on every endeavor I have undertaken. I will hold off detailing any family stories because it will leave me with some instant fodder if I get the urge to write another book. My brothers

Bruce, David, and Keith have been inspirations to me and have provided several of the quotes and anecdotes found in this book. My thanks to my sister-in-law, Donna, and my nieces, Jennifer and Tracy, for adding some missing elements to our family.

I want to give a special thank you to Dick Herrnstadt for putting his special editing touch on this book. I want to thank the United States Air Force for giving me so many rewarding experiences. Although I was harsh on the Air Force a couple of times in this book, I meant no malice. The Air Force was truly a great experience.

Foreword

Sometimes we are so caught up in what we are doing that we can't see what we're doing. It is similar to "being unable to see the forest for the trees." I want to look at some fundamental aspects of our society and draw conclusions, many of which favor *common sense* over political correctness. I want to look at these fundamentals through the eyes of a critic, a skeptic, a realist, and a dreamer. To get the full effect of this book, you will have to prepare yourself to take a neutral stance. If your mind is closed, some statements will inflame you—particularly if you have been sensitized in a certain area. I am a big believer that people learn best when they can relate new material to something they already know. As such, I have given examples wherever I have been able and have explicated in ways that I hope will help you understand my points.

Prelude

In writing this book, the closest I will come to entering the scientific arena is that I will occasionally make reference to the *majority* as a means of making my point. The *majority* that I will allude to is the simple definition meaning more than half. Otherwise, I will mainly appeal to your *common sense,* a capability that has become increasingly more difficult to exercise over the past forty years. Basic *common sense* has become diluted by vigilantes, technology, special interest groups, politics, religion, radicals, and generation gaps, to name a few. In this book, I am going to try to sort out some cracks in the wall of *common sense.* I want to revive *common sense* to a point where it can stand up to contemporary methods of decision-making.

The five years I taught high school JROTC gave me a lot of the material for this book. By working with high school students, I felt that I was helping to establish a foundation for the next generation. Whenever students came into my classroom, they stood beside their desks at parade rest and remained silent. When the bell rang, the student class leader would call the roll. When a student's name was called, she would come to attention and answer, "Present, sir." Any students that arrived after the tardy bell had to stand at the back of the room. After the roll call was completed, the tardy students would come forward and ask for permission to join the class. We then said the Pledge of Allegiance and the Cadet Honor Code, which states, "I will not lie, steal, or cheat, nor tolerate among us anyone who does." I just wish all public schools could operate this way, but I am certain that the ACLU (American Civil Liberties Union) would denounce this practice as an infringement on students' civil liberties. The ACLU has a history of aggressively defending civil rights. All of the students in my class are there by choice. If they don't want to play by the rules, they can leave. If the classroom methods I use were to become standard routine at schools across the country, I have no doubt that many civil rights groups would intervene and declare that students' rights were being violated. The dissenters would declare that students attend school to learn subject matter, not to stand at attention or to answer, "Present, sir," when the role is called. Even if studies prove that students' academics, self-confidence, and attitude all improve under my system, civil rights activists would condemn my system in favor of unbounded freedom.

Roses or Weeds?

As a society, are we more into smelling the roses or pulling the weeds? When I think of someone who passes by the roses but stops to pull the weeds, I think of someone who is more concerned with trying to impress other people than living a full, productive, happy life.

When you stop to smell the roses, you do so to stimulate your senses. You don't do it for any effect that it might have on other people. You just do it to create your own happiness. It seems to me that too many people pass by the rose garden in favor of impressing their neighbors with their weed-free yard. They are pulling weeds instead of smelling roses for the effect it will have on their neighbors. Some people pull weeds based on a sense of pride, but most weed-pullers do so for the effect it will have on others. Americans seem to be drifting away from the rose philosophy and are moving toward the weed philosophy. We are trying too hard to impress others instead of trying to satisfy our own need for true inner peace. Americans have forgotten how to live in ways that create genuine happiness. We attempt to inject happiness into our lives through thrill-seeking, risk-taking, defying the odds, and winning at all costs. We have become flawed in our obsessive drive to be number one, both as a country and as individuals.

Our society is staring some basic problems right in the face, yet we either cannot recognize them or feel powerless to do anything about them. Citizens of the United States sometimes make the statement, "Our system isn't perfect, but it's still the best in the world." It's the best in the world based on what? If you want to base it on affluence, this statement is correct. If you want to base it on the legal definition of freedom, this statement is correct. Yet as free as we are physically, we are all in mental prisons based on some faulty concepts of freedom. *The only real way to measure the greatness of a society is by the genuine happiness of its people.* Using this criterion, the United States is way down the list of happiest countries of the world.

I read about a sociologist who studied the various cultures of the world in order to determine which society was truly the happiest. His conclusion was that tribes living in the rain forests of South America were the happiest people on Earth. Money is supposed to be a huge motivator, but it means nothing to these tribal people. They don't even know what money is.

They are happy even though they don't have cars, iPods, cell phones, microwave ovens, big screen TV's boats, computers, amusement parks, or casinos. Maybe there is something to the old adage that money can't buy happiness. We could learn a lot from these tribal people.

I came across some more recent information on the Internet that ranked 144 countries on happiness. The U.S. was ranked as the 114th happiest country in the world. Costa Rica was rated as the happiest country. There was a blog associated with this happiness study. The comments were very interesting. After reading a number of blogs, I came to some general conclusions. First, many of the people joining the blog were totally inflexible. Other bloggers were so loyal to the U.S. that they just blew off the 114th ranking. A couple of blogs that caught my attention suggested that you can't get a good read on happiness in the U.S. until you have done some worldwide traveling. Once you see how happy some foreigners are, you begin to realize that we don't experience that same kind of happiness. One of my main goals in this book is to get my arms around a substantial number of things that create our unhappiness, many of them self-inflicted.

I want to stimulate you to think about your country's foundation and belief system. My appeal to you is extensively on a *common sense* level, not an intellectual one. Often times *common sense* and intellect lead you to the same place, but by different paths. Intellect tends to produce methods that are logical, rigid, and positions that are more easily defended in disputes. *Common sense* varies from one person to another. What may seem to be *common sense* to one person is not *common sense* to another person. My definition of *common sense* is people observing what is going on around them, tempering their observations with their own experiences and gut feelings, and coming to some conclusions. This kind of reasoning is often abstract and is especially difficult for people who are cynics, disbelievers, or are big on political correctness and rules. In every company I have worked for, there have been co-workers that believe that a rule, is a rule, is a rule - no exceptions. These lovers of rules give their co-workers a hard time when they catch them skirting the rules in favor of *common sense*. I would like to ask these rules-enforcers one thing. If their leg was cut wide open and I was driving them to the emergency room, do they want me to drive at the speed limit or to drive faster?

Subjects up for scrutiny in this book are the very basics of this country: freedom, equality, our legal system, discrimination, culture, and economics, just to name a few. It is amazing to me how many significant flaws we have in these areas and yet boast how other countries should emulate us. Two main themes you will see repeated over and over in this book are *relativity* and *intent*. Many of today's problems are a function of these two themes. If we can come up with a few ways to improve these aspects on a societal basis, we can create a great deal of genuine happiness.

Part of making one's best effort to create successful outcomes in one's life is making plans and then successfully carrying them out. I define this process as having two parts: *theory* and *the application of theory. Theory* is the planning stage that would create an ideal outcome if implemented correctly under ideal conditions. The *application of theory* incorporates various constraints involved at the time the theory is executed. If theory equated to the application of theory, we would need only one down in football as every play is theorized to score a touchdown.

Oftentimes "eye wash" is the focal point of a proposed theory. We do things for the impressions they will have on others and not because they are legitimate goals. We are not as concerned about fixing problems as we are about influencing others with our supposed prowess in some area.

The Constitution is a fundamental component in creating our happiness or unhappiness. It amazes me how much insight the originators of the Constitution possessed. It is quite remarkable how the elements of the original Constitution have withstood the test of time and still have accurate applications today. I do think the Constitution could use a tune-up in a few areas where time has changed our interpretations of what the framers *intended*. There are areas of the Constitution that were probably crystal clear when it was written but are now subjects of vicious debate. The right to bear arms is an example. As far as selecting a group of people to examine the Constitution and make changes, the Supreme Court seems to be the logical choice. The Supreme Court interprets the Constitution on a daily basis and yet it is often fractured due to the ambivalence of the Constitution in certain areas. How many unanimous votes do you see from the Supreme Court? If the Supreme Court rarely votes unanimously, this might be an indication that the Constitution could use a little adjusting. If the Supreme Court were to do a really good job on re-writing the Constitution, a lot of legal wrangling could be done away with. I am sure that there would be a large contingent of people who think that having a vague Constitution is superior to having one that is more definitive. Having a vague Constitution is their idea of freedom.

If you like rules to add structure to your environment, then the federal government and the military are your kinds of organizations. They are both famous for their laws, rules, and regulations. One determining factor in the greatness of a supervisor (boss) is how he interprets rules and regulations. Some supervisors use the rule of thumb that you *can't* do something unless the regulations specifically state that you can. Other supervisors take the stance that you *can* do something unless the regulations specifically state that you *can't*. What I just described to you is an example of individuals demonstrating the half-full versus half-empty glass analogy. When you interpret a regulation, you should always try to deter- mine the *intent* of the regulation. Try to get inside the minds of the people who wrote the regulations to under- stand what they were trying to accomplish. This insight is what I use to govern my actions. When this same kind of rationale is used to evaluate our Constitution, we often misapply what the framers of the Constitution had in mind. Some misinterpretations of our Constitution allow small factions of people to have too much power. *I am a firm believer that a democracy is founded on the principle that you can't make everybody happy, so make the most people happy by letting the majority rule.* However, some flawed interpretations of our Constitution allow the "tail to wag the dog." A classic example of the "tail wagging the dog" occurred in a town near where I was living at the time. There was a cross on the city seal and it had been that way for over a hundred years. Someone new to town pointed out that this was a violation of the laws separating church and state. The courts became involved in this matter and ruled that the cross had to be removed. During the time this issue was going through the courts, a citizen in the community took it upon herself to take a poll to see what the residents thought. Ninety-five percent of the residents wanted to keep the cross on the city seal; however, the small minority of five percent was able to get their way. If you were to ask the group comprising five percent why they made a big deal out of the cross on the city seal, a likely response would be that they felt very strongly about this issue. There are a lot more people among the ninety-five percent that feel equally strong about this issue and the numbers are on their side.

If I were among the five percent—even if I disapproved of the cross because I was of another religion, or an atheist or agnostic—I would not favor my desires over the desires of ninety-five percent of the community. There are many situations like this where a small minority can dictate to a sizeable majority. I don't know what any of us can do to circumvent these kinds of situations. Ego-centric people are generally not very pliable.

By rendering rulings in favor of small groups, judges are giving credence to hypersensitive people. This creates problems where none need exist. Our society is full of hypersensitive and over reacting people. Just to be fair, our society is also full of insensitive people. When we cater to hypersensitive people, we establish precedence that is difficult to live with. We need to take the opinions of hypersensitive people into consideration but ensure that they are tempered with a lot of *common sense.*

Look at the ruckus created about the Pledge of Allegiance. If I were an atheist or agnostic, I would not try to get *God* deleted from the pledge knowing that the vast majority of people favor keeping God in the pledge. It's another case of the minority trying to outdo the majority for power and self-gratification. This country is founded on God. References are made to God on our money, the Pledge of Allegiance, the Declaration of Independence, and many other places. Does it have to get to the point where there is no mention of God anywhere in the government to ensure the separation of church and state? If that is the case, the Constitution needs some revising to make it work the way the framers *intended.*

The following quote is from the U.S. Constitution; First Amendment:

> Congress shall make no law respecting an establishment of religion, or prohibiting the free exercise thereof; or abridging the freedom of speech, or of the press; or the right of the people peaceably to assemble, and to petition the government for a redress of grievances. Congress shall make no law respecting an establishment of religion, or prohibiting the free exercise thereof; or abridging the freedom of speech, or of the press; or the right of the people peaceably to assemble, and to petition the government for a redress of grievance.

The word *separation* cannot be found in the First Amendment yet everybody talks about it like it is. Here is my interpretation of the First Amendment regarding the separation of church and state. To arrive at my interpretation, I tried to put myself into the mindset of the framers of the Constitution. It seems that their intent was to keep the state out of the church so that people could exercise their right to religious freedom. One of the prominent reasons why English people emigrated to America was to have religious freedom. They wanted to be able to practice religion without interference from the government. What is happening now is that there is a big push to get religion out of the government. I believe that the intent of the First Amendment is to keep the government out of religion but not to keep religion out of the government. Why would the framers of the Constitution design the First Amendment to keep the church out of the state and then put references to God everywhere within the government? It is apparent to me that they wanted the separation of church and state to be a one-way street—to keep the state out of the church.

Another battle ground with its roots in the Constitution is the issue of gun rights. The issue of gun rights seems to get more animated and controversial every year. Jump on board with me as I try to employ some *common sense* on the right to own a gun. I want to lay out the positive and negative reasons to have a gun in your house. There are lots of bad things that can happen by having a gun in your house. Gun owners' attitudes are often pretty similar to teenagers' attitudes about driving a car. They know that bad things can happen, but they feel invulnerable. Bad things can happen, but they hap- pen to other people, not me.

Gun owners have heard about all the bad things that can happen by keeping guns in their houses. I am going to create a virtual ledger and put good reasons to have guns in your house on one side of the ledger and bad reasons for having guns in your house on the other side. On the left side of the ledger are the times you successfully injure, kill, or run off an intruder because you have a gun in your house. On the right side of the ledger are situations where having a gun in your house works against you. One bad situation is when an intruder takes your gun away and shoots you. The intruder is the professional and you are the rookie in these situations. More often than not, intruders are unarmed and are there just for the money. They are hoping that you won't be home; however, you force things into a deadly situation by introducing a gun into the situation. Because you try to shoot the intruder, you force the intruder into a win-lose situation. When you try to kill the intruder, he could take your gun away and kill you. If you hadn't displayed a gun and forced the intruder's hand, you would still be alive.

There are times when children find their parents' guns and it leads to their needless death. There are times that marital arguments turn to gunplay because a gun is available in the heat of the moment. There is the possibility that your child might take your gun to school. There is a chance that you will accidently kill an innocent person because your fear caused you to incorrectly diagnose a situation. I recall a situation when a police- man shot a five-year-old boy to death because the boy was in the shadows and had a toy gun in his hand. The list goes on. The positive reasons for owning a gun are far outweighed by the negative reasons to own a gun. If you need to protect yourself from intruders, get the loudest siren you can buy; if that doesn't get the job done, get a taser, stun gun, or pepper spray.

Let's look at another situation where a small

minority creates anger by favoring their own rights over the rights of most people. When a city desperately needs to build a cross-town expressway to alleviate traffic problems, oftentimes, the only place to build the expressway is through an existing residential area. To build an expressway through a residential neighborhood often requires approval from the residents who will be displaced. Invariably, there are some residents that are *unwilling* to sell their property, even at an elevated price; and the proposed expressway goes down the drain. This is a case where a handful of people are able to dictate to an entire city. In some situations, there is a way for the government to overcome these individuals. There is a law called *eminent domain*, which allows the government to overrule the rights of the homeowners and force the sale of their homes. The *eminent domain* law reads like this: "The right of a government to appropriate private property for public use, usually with compensation to the owner." *http://dictionary.reference.com/browse/eminentdomain* (accessed: April 25, 2010). It is human nature to resist change. Change makes people feel uncertain, less confident, and out of sync. We live in a society that prides itself on change. Let's look at an example of what change does to laboratory rats. A colony of rats was taught a societal system that was very rigid. The rats did exceptionally well in this environment. Next the rats' social system was altered and the results were monitored. The rats slowly adapted to their new society norms. This scenario was repeated again and again until the rats eventually went insane. Human beings might be more resilient than rats, but the principle remains the same. Part of what makes people feel secure and confident is living in a society that makes changes in doses the human psyche can handle. Our society has abandoned the concept of inner peace and security in favor of change, particularly change that creates wealth. Constant change is a major impediment to our feelings of security. The rate of change in this country is accelerating in an out of control fashion. Changes during the last forty years, prompted mostly by new technology, have outdone all the changes the world has previously experienced. When money is to be made, you can expect change to happen.

Money stimulates change. Changes in technology are a root cause of creating insecurity. New gadgets come and go or become outdated in such a way that people are left bewildered. Each generation is looking less and less to the past to understand how to live their lives and is more into predicting the future as a source of guidance.

I have a metaphor that I would like to describe for you that speaks to some of the pressure we all feel. Let's say that you walk down a six-inch-wide beam that is one foot off the ground. You feel perfectly comfortable. Now let's put this same beam one thousand feet in the air and have you walk down it. You are scared to death. The only difference is that you have nothing at stake in the first instance while your life is at stake in the second instance. Modern life is much the same way. The more we advance our standard of living, the higher we are raising the "society beam." Concepts like "raising the bar," or "pushing the envelope," or "doing more with less," or "being proactive" are all methods of raising the "society beam." Raising the "society beam" creates additional fear and stress. We need to look for some ways to lower the "society beam" to create a world we all want to live in.

If you go back two hundred years, when a family's house burned down, it was not that big of a problem. It simply created a social gathering to build you a new house. If your house burns down today, it is an extremely traumatic experience. You lose your computer hard drive, your CD's and DVD's, and all your pictures and mementos. You may lose financially by not having enough insurance on your home. The burning of your house now versus then is a totally different experience. Such is true of so many things in our modern society. We feel so vulnerable to losing "things." The Bible speaks very well to this issue, but we can't seem to comprehend it. Even if we could comprehend that we are better off by not possessing so many gadgets, I am doubtful about our ability to give them up. Life is full of things we know are bad for us, yet we continue to let them occupy our time. TV is just such an example. It is not that difficult to rationalize that we might all be better off without TV. It is not just the quality of the TV shows that contribute to our downfall but also the amount of time TV takes away from our relationships, hobbies, chores, and exercising. It would be interesting to see what people would do with their extra time if we took TV away from them. Initially, I would say that a large number of people would suffer from withdrawal and go into a depressed and anxiety- ridden state. Many people would substitute destructive activities for the time they used to spend in front of the TV.

Government, Corporations, And Other Things

I recall four firefighters dying while fighting a forest fire in the state of Washington. The fire that killed them could have been contained much sooner and likely saved these men's lives; however, the lake right next to the fire was home to an endangered species. As such, permission to use the water for fire-fighting had to come from the federal government. While awaiting an answer from the government, these four firefighters were lost to the fire. In a situation like this, I would apply the principle, "It is easier to ask for forgiveness than it is to ask for permission." I would have used the water without gaining permission and figured out the rest later. Protecting fish and animals to the extent that they become more important than people is wrong. Nobody seems to know when the federal deficit will go completely out of control and ruin us as a country.

Will it be a slow process where we can see it coming, or will it completely blindside us? It seems more likely that the federal deficit will blind- side us. Can it be any other way if we cannot define at what point the deficit is truly problematic? Our government has a lot of parallels to businesses that have gone bankrupt. Companies often appear to be doing very well right up to the point of declaring bankruptcy. China is the key player in financing our federal deficit. If they decide to quit financing our federal deficit, we would be in big trouble. I guess our trump card if we get into severe trouble is to call up other countries and give them a message. To Japan, we would say, "Hey, you know that land you own in California and Hawaii? You don't own it anymore!" To China, we would say, "Hey, you know those T-bills and bonds you bought from us? Put them in the trash. We're not going to honor them!"

Nobody knows how much government debt it will take before we have a devastating problem. Things can look rosy, and then the bottom drops out. At what point does the national debt go from being a problem we can handle to one that is out of control? I once heard a tele- vision commentator try to equate the national debt to a mortgage. He likened the debt to a $200,000 house that had only a $20,000 mortgage on it. The homeowner should feel pretty secure. There is one flaw in his analogy. The federal debt is not being paid down every month like a mortgage. It is going up. Would you feel secure if your mortgage was going up every month instead of down, particularly if your house was depreciating? Another statement that is supposed to allay our fears about the national debt is that the government owns trillions and trillions of dollars in assets. If the government gets into dire financial straits, it could just start selling off assets to pay down the debt. I wonder how much we could get for Yellowstone National Park? The problem with this theory is that by the time the government is in such dire straits that it has to sell off assets, everybody else will already have gone under. The government will be the last to go.

The government, in many ways, operates like a giant corporation with the exception that the government has the power to print money. There are a number of one-time maneuvers that companies can do to stave off financial ruin. Let's say that my corporation is deeply in debt to a number of companies. My corporation doesn't have the cash to pay these companies, so I work out a deal to pay them with my corporation's stock. If these other companies agree to my offer, my corporation gets out of debt and increases its outstanding shares of stock at the same time. What a great concept.

Corporate accountants have some maneuvers that they can use on a one-time basis to make things look better than they are. They can arbitrarily write-up or write- down the value of their assets based on borderline justifications. They can shift expenses and revenue from the end of one accounting period into the next accounting period, or they can move expenses and revenue backward from the next accounting period into the current period. What these companies are doing in these situations is to make the current financial statements look better, usually to the detriment of future financial statements.

People can do the same type of thing. It has become commonplace for taxpayers to make thirteen mortgage payments in one year by accelerating January's payment into December. This increases their mortgage interest deduction for the current year and lowers their income tax. However, this maneuver only puts a band-aid on their tax situation. It leaves them with only eleven mortgage payments for the following year. They can execute the same maneuver the following year, but this time it will only be accelerating eleven payments into twelve.

In corporate America, CEO's, COO's, and CFO's devise similar maneuvers that enhance the company's current financial picture but often to the detriment of their financial future. This ritual of maneuvering to benefit the present to the detriment of the future usually gets caught up in a reality check at some point. The corporation can go from being in great financial shape to being in terrible shape very quickly. The CEO's, COO's, and CFO's who maneuvered so beautifully for years to keep their companies artificially afloat are out of maneuvers and can see bad times coming. These company "loyalists" escape with their golden parachutes and watch from afar while the company collapses.

Freedom

The checks and balances built into our federal government are truly works of art. One reservation I have about our political system is that we allow people to vote who know absolutely nothing about politics. I understand our constitutional policy of one person, one vote; however, we force people to get licenses for many things to prove they are competent before we turn them loose. I'm refer- ring to things like driving a car, working as a doctor, or building a dam. I want to entertain you for a few minutes to help you decide whether or not citizens should be required to get a voting license.

One of my favorite segments on The Tonight Show is a segment called "Jay Walking." Jay goes out to the streets and asks people simple questions about history, geography, politics, geometry, etc. I have no idea if the show aired only the dumbest responses or if they air an honest sampling of the responses. Here are some of the responses given to questions posed by Jay: people thought that Chicago was a state; they could not identify a picture of Mount Rushmore; they did not know what Paul Revere was famous for; and they could not locate Africa on a world map. When people were asked to name the vice president of the United States, most people did not know the answer. Some people were shown a picture of Dick Cheney and asked to identify him. Most people could not identify Dick Cheney from his picture. When these same people were shown a number of pictures of Hollywood celebrities, they could name almost all of them.

If you agree with my next statement, I will assume that you are on board with me about requiring a license to vote. *I submit to you that there are more registered voters that can name six brands of beer than can name the two senators representing their state in Congress.* Maybe it's time to require people to pass some sort of qualification test in order to vote. The test would not have to be difficult and would weed out only the people who demonstrate almost no competency in our political system. Voting is a right we give to U.S. citizens just because they are alive. There are no other requirements. If you can breathe and are old enough, you can vote.

When there are really tight political races, politically uninformed people can be the determining factor. I want you to think about this scenario. There is a voter who has learned everything he can about the candidates and the propositions on the ballot. He has watched the debates on TV, he has read newspaper and magazine articles about the candidates, and he has read each party's platform. After gaining all this knowledge about the candidates, he goes to the polls and votes for "candidate A." Another guy in the polling booth next to him has absolutely no knowledge about any of the candidates or propositions on the ballot. He mentally tosses a coin and then votes for "candidate B." He has just nullified the vote of the highly informed voter. I suppose that statistically, the outcome of the election is swayed only slightly because people that mentally toss a coin end up with half voting for "candidate A" and half for "candidate B."

There will always be flaws in our voting system. The position of a candidate's name on the ballot has an effect on how people vote. It shouldn't, but it does. Being listed at or near the top of a list of candidates is a substantial advantage. A candidate's name has a huge impact on the election results. Let's say that a candidate named John Wayne is running against a candidate named Allen Hitler. Is there any doubt about which candidate will win? Even if Allen Hitler is the far superior candidate, he cannot get elected because of his name. Even if John Wayne is an alcoholic who dropped out of school in the fifth grade, he will win the election because of his name. In the upcoming local elections in my town, there is a candidate named Paul Newman. His opponent doesn't have a chance.

One thing I learned a couple of years ago is that voting is not a memory test. It is an open-book test if you want it to be. There is nothing to keep you from taking anything you want into the voting booth with you. I have a friend who does "practice voting" on the sample ballot published in the newspaper. He then takes his filled-out sample ballot with him to the polls. By using this method, his voting is faster and more reliable than other voters. His votes are more reliable because he can use all of his resources at home and become comfortable with his votes. When he effectively votes the day before the election, he can take all the time he needs and feels no pressure at all. In a voting booth, there is a choke factor because it feels like you are taking a test. The long lines waiting to vote will tend to influence you to vote quicker. Maybe you should think about making voting an open-book test.

I want to give you my interpretation of what constitutes a society. My interpretation of a society is a large group of people that have similar ideas, methods of living, customs and traditions, and have some common basis of thinking. When you get away from these principles, you no longer have a society but instead have a large group of individuals. The American society has broken down to the point that we now have a bunch of individuals. We have done this in the name of increasing our freedoms. Today, many people live their lives in ways that disconnect them from cultural norms and the society mainstream. If you go back prior to 1960, there was society pressure on everyone to conform. It was very difficult to get a good job if you were a non-conformist. Today, I see people with purple hair and gaudy tattoos, wearing their pants six inches below their hips. These types of people are expressing the freedoms guaranteed to them by the Constitution. They would have been complete outcasts prior to 1960.

The American society began a major shift in the 1960s that has undermined our country ever since. The beginning of this shift toward unbridled freedom began with the hippie movement. The hippies made the point that you don't have to be a conformist. They seemed to think that the more splintered a society is, the more freedom people have, and the happier people are. It is interesting now when I see TV documentaries about the hippie movement. It seems that most of the hippies eventually came to a crossroads in their life. They realized that continuing to express their radical freedoms beyond their teens and early twenties would cost them financially. Too many employers exercised prejudice and stereotyping against the hippies, which made it difficult for them to get good jobs. The alternative choice for hippies was to once again become conformists and drop back into society. A lot of today's top businessmen are reformed hippies who opted to drop back into society. There are lots of hippies who chose to remain non-conformist, defied the odds, and won; however, I still see some old hippies that impress me as not knowing that the Vietnam War is over. The counter-culture movement is a case where freedom worked against a lot of people.

Americans seem to believe the proposition that increases in freedom translate to increases in happiness.

Is it possible for a society to have too much freedom? It is a certainty from my point of view. Rain is very good, but too much rain causes a flood. Sunlight is very good, but too much sun withers the crops. The same holds true of freedom. I see a lot of instances of people expressing an attitude that they don't have to do anything they don't want to because freedom grants them this right. I hear people talk about "my rights" in ways that indicate that they think their rights are superior to other people's rights. These people have gotten to the point where they express too much freedom, and the way they exercise their freedom is a bother to us all.

A person once painted his house pink and purple as an exhibition of his rights. His neighbors were up in arms. Does the Constitution give people the right to paint their houses pink and purple? On the surface the answer is yes. Freedom as described in the Constitution says that you should be able to paint your house any way you want. This situation ended up going to the courts for resolution. The courts ruled that when your neighbor does something to his property that lowers the value of your property, or has a negative effect on your ability to sell your property, he has damaged you and you have cause for recourse; no more pink or purple houses. The courts were able to rectify this situation, but there are plenty of situations where the courts have ruled in favor of non-conformists in some stunning decisions.

The courts have been heavily involved in finding the middle ground on the smokers' rights issue. I think the courts have done a splendid job validating the rights of both sides. At the onset of this issue, people had always been able to smoke wherever and whenever they desired and nobody had any recourse. Then something happened to change everything. Studies demonstrated that non- smokers can be harmed by secondhand smoke. Non- smokers started to get organized and made their point that smokers' rights stopped where their rights started. The non-smokers declared that they had the right to breathe the smoke-free air. The courts offered a compromise that protected the rights of both sides. Smokers are allowed to smoke, but only in designated areas; and the non-smokers are allowed to breathe clean air. This seemed to be the perfect middle ground. The courts handled this smoking issue in a fair manner, respecting the rights of both smokers and non-smokers.

After all the effort put in by both sides to make things fair, non-smokers have started to mess things up. California decided to ban smoking at the beaches. My question is this: Is smoke the real concern on this issue, or is it something else, like cigarette butts littering the beach, or smokers setting a bad example for children? If the real concern is about peripheral issues, the law should be specific about these issues and not try to disguise them as smoking issues.

A California town named Belmont has set the smoking issue ablaze again. Belmont adopted an ordinance to deny people the right to smoke in their apartments if they share walls with other renters. I find it hard to believe that contaminates coming through the wall are worse than contaminates you breathe when you go out- doors. This ordinance has destroyed the middle ground in favor of non-smokers. No matter how this law is modified, the middle ground has been breached until this law is appealed in its entirety.

I took time to read most of the new California laws regarding smoking. Most of the laws were city ordinances, not state laws. The gist of what I learned is that many municipalities have eliminated virtually every possible place to smoke. When you are not allowed to smoke outdoors or indoors, the laws have become ridiculous.

It is a person's First Amendment right to burn the American flag; however, as a patriot and a veteran, I do not want to have our flag burned, particularly in my presence. Do I have any rights? Where is the middle ground? Is the middle ground to allow the flag burner to burn the American flag but not where patriots are present—let's say in his backyard? On the contrary, is it okay for the protester to burn the flag in public and as the patriot, I should leave if I don't want to watch Old Glory burn? Trying to honor both parties' rights simultaneously is not easy in this situation.

I have another issue where the two sides are far apart in their thinking. Rap music has created contempt and distain in many people who think it is too offensive to be played in public. Other people think that rap music is just a function of freedom and has no boundaries. I am a believer that rap music has a negative effect on people and I have to live in a society with these affected people. When I watched my high school students get into their rap music, it seemed that they were becoming more and more desensitized to the world around them. Is it possible for them to hear words like "cop killer" over and over and yet maintain a healthy perspective on law abidance? Oftentimes, my students would have a really great rap song (in their opinion) and they would want me to listen to it. I told them that I would listen to their song until I heard profanity, a sexual innuendo, or an anti-society statement; and then I would quit. I never had to listen for longer than twenty seconds. These kids are so used to profanity that they don't even recognize it in their songs. With tongue in cheek, I told my students that people who use foul language do so because they have a limited vocabulary. They can't think of an appropriate adjective to use, so they throw in a four-letter word to substitute.

One of the things my students did that drove me crazy was using the same words over and over and over. One of their favorite sayings was *gay.* They also overused *cherry* and "*messed up,*" but *gay* is the one that had to stop. I was tired of hearing that word every day, so I made a rule that I didn't want anybody using that word in my presence. I asked my students to substitute another word for the word *gay.* The students argued vehemently that there was nothing wrong with the word *gay.* I explained to them that I was not banning the word because of its connotations but because they were grossly overusing it. I followed this up by stating that if they were to overuse the word *watermelon,* I would ban it too. You would not believe how often I heard the word *watermelon* the rest of the year, but I hardly ever heard the word *gay*.

Our Constitution grants us enormous freedoms. You can do practically anything, go anywhere, dress any way you want, do whatever job you want, and do things that are extremely immoral (but not illegal). What I want to get across is that *people can have too many choices*. Oftentimes, the choices are mind-boggling. When there are hundreds of choices, people will come away feeling like they may not have made the best choice. It is human nature to think that one of your other choices would have been better. No matter which choice you pick, you will wish that you had picked a different one. This might happen quickly or it might take some time for the feeling to sink in, but it will happen quite often. This illustration might speak to why people change jobs so often, move so often, and get divorced so often. There are so many choices that inevitably one of their other choices will start looking better to them. Once people get in the habit of retreating to another choice when things get tough, loyalty and trust are abandoned. Granted, you don't want to live in a society where you have no choice or maybe only one choice. This is the other extreme, and this situation is not the answer either. In my opinion, the average person functions best if they have three to five choices to consider. If your first choice doesn't work out, you can go on to your second choice and become reasonably satisfied. In today's society, the large number of choices can cause people to have a difficult time finding a choice they are really comfortable with. I don't know how the average high school or college graduate knows how to make a decision about what to do next. Too many choices! It was certainly easier in my day when I had only a limited number of choices.

Do modern inventions really serve to make us happy? Let's take the example of a person who buys a new Porsche. He parks his car at the far end of the parking lot to avoid getting dings from surrounding parked cars. He puts a cover over his car to avoid the damaging rays of the sun. He wants his boss to be understanding when he bolts from work at the slightest threat of a storm. The guy who owns a Porsche and then acts this way is pulling way too many weeds and not smelling enough roses. I think people who drive reliable, moderate-looking cars are happier than Porsche owners. They have greater peace of mind by not having to worry about where everybody else is parking or what the weather is doing.

Equality

Equality is a tough subject to approach because no matter what kind of stance I take, I will enflame somebody. When I refer to equality, I am referring to all cross- segments of our society. I will not just be talking about gender, race, religion, etc. I will also be talking about parent-child relationships, student-teacher relation- ships, co-worker relationships, and other relationships that are not usually spoken about on a societal level.

Is it possible to have too much equality in a society just like you can have too much freedom? Fasten your safety belts and I will lead you down the highway of equality. I have lots of examples for you to examine and decide for yourself what equality means to you.

It is now considered okay for married women to retain their maiden name or even take on a hyphenated name like Smith-Martin. As a result, lots of children now have hyphenated last names. What is supposed to happen when those children marry another person with a hyphenated last name? Are the offspring of this couple going to have four hyphenated last names, and is it possible that the next generation could have eight sur- names? Get ready for a flock of by-products that are a function of the equality movement.

It seems that there are vigilantes for every cause in America. Some of them make good watchdogs and keep things moving in the right direction. There are also vigilantes who seem to be trying to make a name for themselves at the expense of our society. If you knew everything about every person, you would be shocked and appalled at human nature. The things we do as individuals are truly shocking. Let me give you one piece of advice. If you ever undergo a polygraph examination and are asked, "Is there anything you have ever done to discredit yourself," make sure that you answer yes. Your subconscious will start thinking about the times you cheated on a test, peeked in a window, or lied to your parents or spouse.

Let's suppose that you discovered some information about Billy Graham that would ruin his reputation and you were the only one in possession of this information. Would you divulge this information to the public or would you just tuck it away? If you go back fifty years, people were not inclined to publicize this kind of information. It was assumed that we all have "dirty laundry," so let's keep it to ourselves. When star athletes were caught in immoral situations, the media did their best to keep it under wraps. It doesn't work that way anymore. People will divulge dirty laundry and feel that they are doing society a favor.

There are very few, if any, true American heroes any- more. I grew up idolizing many heroes; some of them were real, and some were TV characters. Some of my heroes were people like policemen, teachers, distinguished students, ministers, and athletes. My TV heroes were people like Superman, The Lone Ranger, Marshall Dillon, and Hoss Cartwright. Having heroes is good for people. The media are always looking to bring people down from high places. That's what the ratings game is all about. Look at all the priests that have "fallen on their swords." Dozens of politicians have been caught taking the moral low road. Company CEO's as a whole are looked upon with disdain. The actions of a few people have caused our society to significantly lower their respect for entire professions.

What would the world be like if everyone were given equal status? Let's start with a premise that everyone has equal stature. Children are equal to adults. Everyday citizens are equal to judges and policemen. Students are equal to teachers and principals. This obviously would not work. There would be total chaos. People would misuse the system for their own advantage. Total equality would be a mess. What would happen if all employees were totally equal? The arguing and fussing at work would be terrible. There would be a bunch of self-appointed bosses. Employees would be at a loss as to what to do and who to follow. There are some aspects of life where inequality works best.

I remember the day when people had total respect for the police. When you got pulled over for speeding, there was a lot of "Yes, sir," and "I'm sorry, sir," and "I won't let it happen again, sir." Today, the police officers hear, "I didn't do it," and "Your radar gun is off," and "Everybody else is doing it. Why pick on me?" So what happened to create this change? We found some individuals within the law enforcement profession who did not live up to their code of conduct. We transferred this fact to the entire profession, thus taking the entire profession down a few notches. This is called stereotyping. We have done the same thing to other professions as well. Some people would say that the punishment fits the crime and that we all have a responsibility to take down people and professions that are not living up to their billing. There is a difference between holding individuals accountable and trying to discredit entire groups of people associated with them. This type of action, called projection, is a cornerstone in the erosion of respect in this country.

A number of Los Angeles police officers committed misdeeds that they vehemently denied until video tapes emerged that discredited them. The actions of these police officers have severely damaged the credibility of the Los Angeles Police Department and have served to damage the credibility of police officers everywhere.

The Catholic Church is trying to recover from the negative publicity created by sexual misconduct by some priests. People will naturally wonder if these priests are just the tip of the iceberg. Some people will expand on the current information and extrapolate that there are hundreds of priests that are just as guilty but haven't been caught. Here is the bottom line for this entire scenario: only a small percentage of all priests have been caught in sexual misconduct, but the media presentations make people feel like the number is much higher. The result of all the negative publicity is that the Catholic Church and its priests are now looked at in a different light. I shudder when I think what would happen if the Pope was ever caught in some misdeed. I'm not sure the Catholic Church would be able to remain viable.

It's time for me to shift gears. Our society norms now consider it okay to call our doctors, lawyers, ministers, bosses, teachers, and bankers by their first name. Even children call these professionals by their first name. To help understand the effects of calling doctors, clergy, or other professionals by their first name, I want to ramp things up a bit. What if people started calling the president or the pope by their first name, ignoring their titles all together? I hope you see this action as a sign of dis- respect, not friendship. With that thought in mind, is there any significance that we should attach to people calling doctors, clergy, police officers, or college professors by their first name? I see the transformation from title and last name (Dr. Smith) to a first-name basis as one more by-product of the equality movement. It breaks down the barrier between highly respected professionals and their clients. I really don't know if this is a plus or a minus. I'm in favor of having children address adults by title and last name in order for them to learn respect. Heroes and their worshippers is an unequal relationship, but it's this inequality that makes it one of the most cherished relationships. The hero and hero worshipper relationship is very powerful. When I was a young boy, it brought me great pleasure to worship my heroes. For me to know that my local heroes were willing to acknowledge me when I was around them was a "kick in the pants." I felt special. I was fortunate enough later in my life to turn the tables and assume the role of the hero. By playing sports in high school and college and flying airplanes in the Air Force, I created a few fans of my own. Being a hero creates a special feeling. It is the lack of equality that creates this special relationship. The hero worshipper gets to worship her hero, thus making her feel special; and the hero gets an ego boost from the relationship. It's a super deal for both people. There is definitely a place for respectful, unequal relationships. I'm just not sure these kinds of relationships will survive all of the social upheaval and social engineering that are going on.

When I taught college ROTC, the following situation occurred with regularity. My cadets were required to run a mile and a half for time. When the male cadets ran thirteen minutes, I had to tell them that they didn't have what it takes; and after a second failure, I had to dismiss them from the program. When the female cadets ran the same distance in fourteen minutes, I told them they had done a great job. There are only two sensible resolutions to this discrepancy between male and female standards.

If the mile and a half qualification doesn't mean any- thing, get rid of it. If it is a viable criterion, males and females should be held to the same standard. In the military, the enemy doesn't care what gender they are shooting at. They are going to pick off the slowest runners. A soldier is a soldier, and they all have to perform to very high standards. It is imperative that women be able to perform in sync with men. This is not discrimination. It's making some practical sense out of an equality movement that seeks no boundaries. The same situation exists for policemen and firemen. The person must be able to do the job, and gender has nothing to do with it. What would it be like if there was a word processing job that required fifty words per minute for women but only thirty words per minute for men as a function of placing more men in this career field? You really can't do that. You need to make the standards the same for everyone. To do otherwise is reverse discrimination.

One equality issue that caught fire a few years ago was the unequal pay between men and women at the Wimbledon Tennis Tournament. It is difficult for many people to comprehend that men and women tennis players are not paid identically when they play side-by-side for two weeks. Let's dig a little deeper on this issue by looking at some different methods for determining pay for professional tennis players:

1. Determine pay based on how much time the players actually spend on court. If you use this standard, the 2006 Wimbledon women's winner, Amelie Mauresmo, made twenty-two percent more money than the men's winner, Roger Federer. This discrepancy is created because women play the best of three sets while men play the best of five sets.
2. If you go by ability alone, men tennis players are substantially underpaid. In June 2009, I talked with a former French Open champion who played the tour for more than fifteen years. The question I posed to him was how far down the men's rankings I could go and still find a player that would be number one on the women's tour. He said that it would be conjecture on his part to answer that question but that he had a story that would be more meaningful than the answer I was seeking. He told me that there were two women tennis players who had recently risen to the top of the rankings and felt like world beaters. They got carried away at a post-match press conference and boasted that they could beat the two-hundredth ranked men's player. Much to their chagrin, the two-hundredth ranked man sought them out in short order. He came up to them and said, "Hi. I'm the two-hundredth ranked man in the world. Let's get it on." The matches took place in strict privacy to avoid any potential media frenzy. This man beat

the first woman 6–1 and then beat the second woman 6–2.

3. Finally, if you go by the number of spectators the players put into the seats, men have a decided advantage. It is difficult to make this determination by watching Wimbledon because it is a combined men's and women's tournament. If you look at the attendance figures at women-only or men-only tournaments, you can get a better reading on who is putting spectators into the seats. The men's tour attracts significantly more fans than the women's tour does.

Based on these three factors, should women tennis players be paid equal to men tennis players? I am in favor of equal pay because you cannot base all your decisions by crunching numbers. A sense of fairness and charity would lead one to make the prize money at Wimbledon equal for men and women. I can also see the opposing rationale that just because two people are doing the same thing, at the same place, at the same time, does not necessarily warrant the same pay. Sports are a totally different situation than a typical work place. Look at the situation where two linemen work side-by-side on a professional football team. They do the same things, put out the same effort, and spend an equal amount of time at practice and games. Should these two players be paid the same? They will not be paid the same because one player has more ability than the other.

The pay discrepancy between men and women

in the work place first became an issue a couple of generations ago, and yet progress has been slow. How can that be? The reason this is happening is because women are working against a host of discriminatory factors other than gender. A substantial number of men receive lower pay than other men because they face these same non- gender factors. The equal pay issue is much more complicated than most people think. In the next few para- graphs, I will attempt to explain some factors other than gender that explain unequal pay in the work place.

The following non-gender statements offer alternative explanations as to why women make less pay than men. These statements usually go unrecognized in debates about pay, but they are also factors in unequal pay.

1. Beautiful and handsome people make more money than average-looking people.
2. Graduates of private universities make more money than graduates of public universities.
3. Assertive people make more money than nonassertive people.
4. Tall men make more money than short men.
5. Men with deeper sounding voices make more money than men with higher pitched voices.

These statements are all true. My information for these statements comes from a course I taught at the

University of Phoenix on Contemporary Issues in American Business.

As you can see, there are a number of discriminating factors involving workplace earnings; gender is just one of them. If I derive some logic from the statements above, it seems that women are not only fighting a gender factor for equal pay but they are also fighting height and assertiveness issues. Considering that on average women are shorter than men, women won't get paid the same as men until short men are paid the same as tall men. On the whole, men are more assertive than women. Men will ask their boss for a raise more readily than women will. The assertiveness factor also plays into promotions, another factor that determines pay.

The bottom line is this: until all of the aforementioned discriminators (and many more) can be eradicated, women's pay will never catch up with men's pay. These factors speak to only a few of the non-gender factors affecting unequal pay. There are many more factors, many that have not been identified in any studies. A lot of gender discrimination issues have made significant strides over the past forty years. I hope that I have given you some insight as to why the gender pay issue has evolved at such a slow pace. Society is going to have to solve all the discriminatory factors in order to effectively promote equal pay for everyone. Eventually, there might be more effective laws dealing with the gender aspect of pay. I doubt, however, that there will ever be effective anti-discrimination laws about height, looks, assertiveness, or where one went to college. It seems that there will always be some invalid workplace discriminators that are too complex to be rectified. You would have to change human nature to fix all workplace discrimination, and this is not possible.

As a country, we need to define equality in some ways that make sense. It seems to me that unbridled equality makes no sense. Bums and scholars are not equal except in the Constitutional definition of equality. Other than the Constitutional applications, equality should be something you earn, not just have bestowed upon you. Please read on as I break down various arenas of equality and inequality.

Let's begin with the basic premise that "all men are created equal." My interpretation of this definition is that when you are born, all the doors of life are open to you. Where you go from there is your responsibility. Some of us will start closing doors almost immediately. Some people will choose paths that lead to prison; other people will choose paths that lead to successful careers. The theory is that we all get to the starting line equally. This means that some people will need an extra boost to get to the starting line with everyone else. It does not mean that we all get to the finish line equally. Where you finish is your responsibility. Some people will have to work harder than others to get to the same level because they start out with social handicaps. I am talking about things such as being born into poverty or going to sub- standard schools. If you find yourself in this situation, you must be receptive to the idea that you will have to work harder to achieve at the same level as more fortunate people. If that sacrifice is made, the cycle can be broken for future generations.

As a society, we have invented ways for people to get to the finish line without having to work for it. Some of the equal opportunity laws were established to give certain groups a jump-start to make up for all the suffering and oppression endured by previous generations that have put them at a disadvantage now. These laws had very good intentions when they were first introduced; however, to select somebody who is way down the list of applicants over someone who is higher up is reverse discrimination, and I am not sure this is the best solution to the problem. I'm not sure what kind of laws we can enact that protect the rights of oppressed individuals to move forward that are also fair to people that have worked hard to separate themselves from the crowd. I have seen videotapes of firefighter applicants trying to pass the physical standards tests. Some of them couldn't scale a four-foot wall. Some of them couldn't carry a person out of a burning building. Some of them couldn't climb a ladder, yet these people were hired because of equal opportunity laws. This is a tough issue to handle. The laws need to assist certain groups to get them on the right track, but reverse discrimination is also a problem. In a situation like firefighting, you have to pick the most qualified applicants because people's lives are at stake. Equal employment opportunity laws have to be tempered for situations like this. Many people think that equal opportunity laws have served their purpose and are either obsolete or are creating reverse discrimination. We need to be more creative in order to solve perpetual social problems instead of employing a problem substitution tactic.

A considerable number of people are proclaiming that the time has come for people to stand on their own two feet and be accountable for where they end up in life. Admittedly, it is going to be tougher on people whose family history or culture works against them. Equality is a tough thing to define; but I feel that it is meant to get people to the starting line together, not the finish line.

It is interesting how people view human rights violations of the past. Today, we apply an entirely different set of standards for evaluating human rights than the standards that were in place a few decades ago. By today's standards, spanking children is considered child abuse by many people and organizations. Parents of the spanking era did not see anything wrong with their actions, and many lament the fact that society has taken away spanking as a viable form of attitude adjustment.

In 1992 I did a little research to determine to what extent women from the 1950s realized in real time that they were being oppressed. I quizzed my grandmother and some of her elderly friends to learn if they had realized during the 1950s that they were being oppressed or abused. They spoke in unison that the only thing they knew at that time is that they were doing the same things that their mothers and grandmothers had done.

They didn't see themselves as being oppressed. It is only in retrospect that they see things in a different way.

I have another touchy subject to present. There is a movement in our society to open private organizations for all who want to join. Many of these organizations were formed to create a certain type of atmosphere that the members want. When outsiders that don't fit the mold join these types of organizations, they ruin the established atmosphere. There is a definite place for all-men's or all-women's organizations. Some organizations just don't have the same flavor when a member of the opposite sex is present. Social organizations are often formed for the purpose of promoting a particular atmosphere. This atmosphere is created to enhance a certain kind of bonding or fellowship. Are we at a point where we can no longer have organizations that exclude people who do not fit the mold? Should a baldheaded men's organization be forced to admit men with long hair? Should MENSA be forced to admit people of all intelligences? Should retired groups be forced to admit younger people?

It is important to have organizations that cater to select groups of people. Being with people that have similar characteristics and interests enhances friendships and bonding. All-male or all-female organizations are often the most cherished groups. There is a flavor to these groups that can't be achieved by having by having mixed company. It's maddening to think that organizations should be forced to open their doors to all people, yet there are people who are campaigning for laws that would do just that. Organizations should not be forced to admit people that don't fit the organizational image just to prove that they do not discriminate. I personally do not have a problem with private organizations running their business the way they want to as long as they don't break the law or bother anyone. Admitting people who do not fit the mold changes the flavor of a group. Remember when I said that one person's rights stop where another person's rights start? This rationale applies to private organizations as well as individuals. As much as people think that they have the right to join a private organization, the organization should retain the right to exclude people who would substantially change the atmosphere of the organization. To support a person's individual rights over the rights of an organization is another example of a lesser number of people dictating to a larger number of people. It shouldn't be that way. To make one person happy at the expense of an entire group doesn't pass the common sense test. As for public organizations, they are a different story. Anyone should be allowed to join any public organization with a few exceptions. I don't think non-alcoholics should be able to attend Alcoholics Anonymous (AA) meetings even though AA is considered to be a public organization. Admitting outsiders to AA meetings would have an indelible impact on the atmosphere and this could upset the program.

If you can believe it, there are still some private, all-male golf clubs in America. Probably the most exclusive private golf club in the world is the Augusta National

Golf Club (home of the Masters Golf Tournament). The National Organization for Women (NOW) has made cracking this club a stated goal. The flavor of this club will change drastically if women are admitted. It will become a real-life example of the dialogue I just presented. The current members of the club will become less happy, and the women that join the club will not be happy either. It will be a lose-lose situation promoted by politics. People's happiness and best interests are at stake. The first female members might not even spend time at the club because of their realization that they don't fit in.

If this scenario about a private golf club doesn't go far enough in convincing you that private clubs should not be forced to be politically correct, I have a real-life story that puts everything in perspective. When I was in the Air Force, there was an association called the Officers' Wives' Club. I recall a huge fuss that arose when the husband of an Air Force officer tried to join the Officers' Wives' Club. The colonels' wives went crazy. This situation was in turmoil for six months. Finally, the legal interpretation of equality won out and this gentleman was approved for admission. His admission would surely have changed the flavor of the club in a dreadful way, but at least the organization would be politically correct. This guy never had any intention of joining the club. He just wanted to prove how political correctness can really mess things up. He proved that just one outsider in a closed organization can ruin the atmosphere. Phooey with political correctness and hurray for common sense!

I recall a couple of occasions where TV commentators made statements that were essentially correct but not politically correct, and it cost them their jobs. One such case was that of Jimmy "The Greek" Snyder who was a pro football analyst for CBS. He gave his analyses of why blacks could run faster and jump higher than whites. Political correctness says that you can't do that, and he was fired. Here are some factors that make his statement a truism, but only if you look at them with an open mind:

1. Black people's heritage is Africa. For thousands of years, Africans were forced to run and jump to catch prey or to keep from becoming prey. It seems reasonable that this regimen developed stronger running and jumping genes. White people came from Europe, where there was never the same mandate to run and jump. The Olympics validate my point emphatically. If you look back at the last five Olympics, the hundred-meter medal races have consisted of only black runners. There has not been a single white participant in the hundred-meter medal race for over twenty years. To add some additional credence to this analysis, blacks in these races came from all over the world, not just the better training facilities offered in the U.S. I do not want to diminish all the hard work, dedication,

and sacrifice that blacks put in to enhance their natural abilities. Genes alone are not going to elevate a person to the top of their sport. I want to pay due diligence to black athletes for advancing their natural talent.

2. Many black athletes come from poor, inner-city neighborhoods. There is a distinct cultural inducement in these neighborhoods for children to get involved in sports. These children feel that athletics is their best possible ticket out of the inner city.
3. Of the literally hundreds of sports, blacks dominate four sports in numbers far beyond their percentage of the population. These four sports are basketball, football, track and field, and boxing. I don't think there is any coincidence that these sports are relatively inexpensive and can be played right in their own neighborhoods. I also do not think it is a mere coincidence that these sports require more running and jumping skills than most other sports do. Question: Was Jimmy "The Greek" Snyder incorrect on his statement? Should Jimmy have been fired for his statement?

Another case where common sense and political correctness were at odds involved Dusty Baker, a black manager of the Chicago Cubs. Dusty spent his entire life in baseball. His personal insight on a certain matter got him into trouble with the politically correct crowd.

He stated that black baseball players could withstand the heat better than white players. Some people came down hard on him for making this statement because he did not have empirical evidence to back his assertion. Based on these facts as presented, Dusty did not violate any basics of common sense, but he violated the basics of political correctness by telling the truth. The races might be equal under the law, but they are not equal in all aspects of human life. This situation is inane and makes you wonder what kind of person would challenge such an obvious conclusion. It seems that there are always some people who enjoy verbal sparring.

Equality under the law refers to people's rights, not their culture or inborn skills. There is a distinct difference between saying that all people have the same rights and saying that all people are the same. After a person's Constitutional equality has been bestowed upon him, it is his responsibility to enhance that equality, not to use it as a shield or a weapon. Get out there and make some- thing of yourself. As a retired military man, I guess I need to take a stance on women in the military. When I think of women in the military, I have very few problems with it. I do have two drawbacks about women being on the front line. Women being on the front lines with men can create sexual tension, a definite obstacle to discipline. This is not to implicate either sex. It is just a natural fact of life. I have no problem with women being killed, taken prisoner, or killing the enemy. Some people do have a problem with women being in these situations. I have one other reservation about putting women on the front lines. When the soldier next to her gets his head blown off, will she be able shake it off and carry on? I have seen enough crying women in my time to realize that women are much more emotional than men. I am not sure that women can be in the front lines with their emotions. The mothering and nurturing aspects of women seem to be a decided liability when fighting on the front lines. Obviously, there are many women who are on par emotionally with men on the front lines. There are also many men who can't do any better than the average woman in this situation. The problem is that it isn't practical to try to determine individually who will stay strong and who will react negatively in these situations. To have the strongest force possible, I would elect to apply the percentages. A higher percentage of men than women will react favorably in these situations. Based on these two factors—sexual tension and negative emotional reaction to combat—I would make the decision to put only men on the front lines. Women can be tremendous assets, but it makes sense to put them in roles where they are equal to or better than men. Women can fly airplanes, serve on ships, provide logistical support, be truck drivers, provide communications, and perform many other jobs. As a coach, this is the play that I would call, realizing full well that the Monday morning quarterbacks are going to have a field day at my expense. War is not the place for political correctness. Go with your best team, even if it is not politically correct.

PRODUCTIVITY

As a country we are continuously trying to develop new methods to raise productivity levels. We have done this to the point of making people miserable. Life isn't about what happens to you, but how you feel about what happens to you. Suppose you give $20 to some worthy charity. You feel really good. Now suppose somebody steals $20 from you. You feel terrible. Either way you are out $20, but the way you feel about being out $20 is totally different. It is much the same way in the workplace. If your boss sets a goal for you of producing 120 units and you produce only 100 units, you feel bad and will likely hear about it from the boss. If your goal had been to produce 90 units and you had produced 100 units, you would feel great. Either way you produced 100 units, but how you feel about producing 100 units is totally different.

Let's say a person who has never made more than minimum wage is hired for a job paying $70,000 per year. He is elated beyond belief. Another person who is used to making $500,000 per year gets downsized into a job that pays $70,000 per year. He is very unhappy. They are both making $70,000 a year, but the way they feel about making $70,000 is totally different. This is the relativity factor. The advances we make as a society can work against us when we apply the relativity factor. The more we achieve, the bigger the fall if we subsequently fail. By raising the bar, we create situations much like the six-inch beam I described earlier. If the beam is one foot off the ground, you can walk down it with confidence. If you walk down this same beam when it is one thousand feet in the air, your confidence wanes and your fear and anxiety increase. The reason your confidence wanes is because you have more to lose if you fail. All the progress and improvements we have made as a society have raised the height of our "individual and society beams." In relative terms, we are all walking a very high beam created by progress. A few hundred years ago the society beam was always low. There wasn't much people could do to elevate themselves. All of the inventions that we use in our daily lives today serve to raise the beam. We have become slaves to "things and stuff." People today go to pieces if their car won't start or they get a scratch on their furniture. It is difficult for workers to feel really good about their accomplishments. When a goal is achieved, the boss simply raises the bar to a higher level and says, "Get back to work." This raising of the bar sends a subtle message to employees that, "You could be doing better." Guess what happens when you keep raising the bar or pushing the envelope to very high standards? You induce cheating as a means of attaining that higher goal. Raising the bar or pushing the envelope to unrealistic levels induces corruption and cheating. Professional sports might well have been the group that invented the term "raising the bar." The larger the reward for winning, the more dishonesty and cheating are induced. New methods of cheating are exposed all the time: corked bats, steroids, spying on the other team's practices, altering documents, fixing games, betting on one's own sport—the list is endless. I recall a poll taken of Olympic athletes that presented them with a hypothetical scenario: The athletes were told that there is an undetectable performance enhancing drug which guarantees the athletes that they will win a gold medal. However, the athletes were also told that this new drug would kill them in five years. The athletes were asked anonymously if they would take the drug under these conditions. Over seventy percent of the athletes said that it was worth dying in five years to win a gold medal today.

There is a pecking order in corporate America for "applying the screws" to different departments within a company to make the company profitable. The first department to be pressured is sales and marketing. If the sales and marketing departments are doing a fantastic job, they will keep the heat off of everyone else. What happens if sales are not getting the job done? The next department in line to feel the pressure is the production department. Hey production people, it's time to scrutinize your department to the max. Sales and marketing aren't getting the job done, so we're going to squeeze you to turn company profits around. If the production department is unable to boost company profitability, it becomes time to find another department that can increase company profits. The onus now falls on the accounting department. When I took accounting in college, I recall it being a method for keeping financial records, not for creating company profit. When a company's first two lines of defense (sales and production) are unable to produce the desired profits, the next department to be pressured is accounting. Accountants are supposed to make things look better financially by using smoke and mirrors. Accountants no longer just keep the books. They are supposed to employ creative accounting to improve the company's bottom line. It's just a matter of time until these companies are discovered for their creative accounting or until things descend to a level where even the accounting department can't resurrect the company.

I hope that you are now convinced that we are all better off living in less productive, less stressful ways. People are ultimately happier when the competitive environment melts away. There are some drawbacks to everybody living an easier, more serene life. The economy will sink like a rock. The economy is so fragile that it can barely withstand small changes. It would not be able to withstand a change like an entire society deciding to live a simpler life. We would live in a never-ending recession induced by our less competitive spirit.

That's okay. You make the decision to live a simpler life. Everybody else makes the same decision. The economy sinks. Everybody makes less money due to the recession. People are living a simpler life and don't need as much money. This whole thing is just a self-fulfilling prophesy. You make less money, you spend less money. There are a lot of other countries living that way that are truly happy. As a country, we don't seem to get it.

I saw a study that indicated that employees are non-productive for approximately an hour and a half per day. This means that they spend this amount of time chat- ting with co-workers, doing personal business on company time, talking on the telephone, going to the break room, and other things that are not productive for the company. The solution, therefore, is to crack the whip on the employees—a day's work for a day's pay—right? I can guarantee you that any employee who never steals time from his employer will become a basket case at some point. Working without stealing any time from your employer while working eight- to ten-hour days, five to six days per week, fifty weeks a year, for forty years will create miserable people. There is another way of looking at this situation. When employees steal time from work, they are indirectly saying that they are feeling too much pressure. If management isn't going to be sensible in setting work hours and conditions, then employees are going to steal time to compensate. If work hours and productivity goals are set at reasonable levels, employees won't need to steal time to keep their sanity.

Of course, there will always be workers who will steal time at work no matter how good you make it for them; however, employers shouldn't penalize the entire work- force for the misdeeds of a few employees.

We all know that employees occasionally call in sick when they are not really sick. I asked a number of people why they do this. Some of them indicated that they were taking a "mental health day." What they were saying was that they needed a day off to reduce the pressure of work. It is sort of like taking a day of prevention as opposed to taking several stress-induced sick days later. We take our cars in for preventative maintenance so we can reduce the chances for an unexpected breakdown. Maybe it's time to allow employees to be up-front with their employers about what they do with their sick days. It seems prudent to me that an employee should be able to call into work and announce that she is taking a "mental health day" without having to disguise or justify it. It's time to recognize that sick days apply to mental health as well as physical health.

You are not stealing time from work if you take a "mental health day." All employees go to work on days they are sick and should have stayed home. When you take a "mental health day," you are just compensating for those days that you went to work when you should have stayed home. For most employees, the number of days they go to work when they are sick far outnumber the days they stay home when they are well. This realization should make you feel less guilty the next time you take a mental health day.

You need to be careful about maximizing your productivity at work. Once you prove you can perform at a certain level, you are expected to maintain that level or even improve on it. This is like expecting a professional golfer to shoot 65 all the time because he has proved that he can do it on a few occasions. Nobody can be expected to maintain their top level of productivity on an ongoing basis. It creates stress that can translate into physical or mental problems. My estimate of what people should be expected to maintain on a long-term basis is about eighty-five percent of their maximum capability. To expect more than that keeps the pressure on and makes employees stressed out.

One reason people change jobs is to get away from workplace personality conflicts. Another reason they quit is because they are stifled in dead-end jobs. A third reason people change jobs is to move up financially. I think most people recognize these factors for changing jobs. There is another prevalent factor that leads to job changes. People quit their jobs just to get additional time away from work, even if it means going without a paycheck for a while. Two weeks of vacation a year is not enough time to recharge their batteries. They need additional time off from work, even if it means having to go without a paycheck while they are between jobs. I once had a boss who told me to never be sick for more than a week. He said that if I was ever gone for more than a week, he would have to hire someone to replace me. Nobody needs that kind of pressure. It's enough to make you sick.

Our free enterprise system is a great way to run an economy. There will always be some flaws in any system, but our system is the best thing going at this time. There is one thing about a free enterprise system that bothers me. You are free; free to be rich or free to be poor. The onus is on you. According to statistics I have seen, the rich are getting richer and the poor are getting poorer. If this trend continues for a long enough time, there will eventually be a class war. The have-nots will get tired of being poor and will decide to go take it from the haves.

The pressure to be number one is killing us as a nation, but we don't know any other way to do it. The pressure of being at the top is making us miserable in the workplace and at home. It causes parents to fight at Little League games. It causes competitors to cheat. Is being number one really the best place to be? As Americans we often use perfection as an instrument for judgment. Suppose your car starts ninety-six percent of the time. You would call it a piece of junk. Ninety-six percent does not cut it. One hundred percent is the standard.

"Doing more with less" is one of the dumbest concepts we ever came up with. After you go through a few rounds of doing more with less, you will arrive at a point where you are doing everything with nothing. Why are we doing more with less in an ongoing basis? From scientific and psychological standpoints, it doesn't make sense. It is merely management's way of squeezing employees for the benefit of the company. "Doing more with less" was designed to be a short-term strategy, but many companies have adopted it as their standard operating procedure. It can't possibly work as a long-term strategy; workers will revolt.

Let's take a look at another area where corporate America is wrecking our personal lives. I find it intriguing that the qualities we esteem most for workers create havoc if exercised in one's personal life. Do we really want dads and husbands to be like General Patton or some company CEO? Let's make a list of some traits that make one hugely successful at work but can be relationship killers when exercised at home: assertiveness, staying on the job until it's done; being an expert; being dogmatic; displaying an unwillingness to lose; working late hours; getting the most out of the people you man-age; being detail-oriented; being a perfectionist. These qualities are great for job productivity and efficiency but will create friction at home if executed in the same manner. When I contrast these great worker qualities with the qualities that make for a great spouse or parent, I see a huge contrast. The personal qualities that make for a special kind of spouse or parent do not make you the most esteemed worker. Traits such as kindness, honesty, integrity, yielding to others, and volunteering your services for no personal gain will make one a great parent or spouse but will likely cost him in the workplace.

Productivity means more than just how much output can be attained. Have you ever thought of credit cards as being a function of productivity? Once you crank up the productivity, you have to find consumers. Hundreds of gimmicks exist for enticing people to buy things they don't need. Credit cards are just such a tactic. What we are really doing is stealing from the future to make the economy look better today. This is a prevalent trend in this country—make things look good now and worry about the future when we get there (if we get there). One of the best marketing gimmicks companies have developed is to play on your self-image. "Hey, you out there. You're miserable. The reason you're miserable is because you don't own our product. If you owned our product, then you would be happy." These advertisements may very well be correct about you being miserable; however, it is doubtful that you are miserable because you don't own the product they are pushing. Your misery stems from elsewhere, but you can't seem to figure it out. Buying this company's product will probably not help your misery, just extend it and make you poorer to boot. Marketers also play on your fears and guilt as strategies for selling their products.

What about the old saying, "Money can't buy happiness"? Some people say that if you believe this statement, you're not shopping at the right places. This statement about money not being able to buy happiness is mostly true. The best things in life are free; however, you need to have a little money in the bank to keep you from being such a nervous wreck that you can't enjoy them. Financial problems impede your ability to enjoy the free things that touch your soul. You need some money to experience a fulfilling life, but an excessive amount of money does not guarantee any greater happiness. Some of the most miserable people are people with lots of money.

A lot can be learned from looking at professional baseball players. Which era of baseball players were hap- pier, the players of the 1940s and 1950s, or the players of the 1990s and 2000s? The ballplayers from the earlier era were paid very little and absolutely loved the game. The pressure was off because of their low pay. Ballplayers today sign high-dollar contracts and then feel pressure to live up to them—another case where money isn't all that it's cracked up to be.

Many people think that if they just had more money, they would be much happier. Money will always be a major concern in one's life regardless of whether one is rich or poor. When you are poor, what keeps you awake at night is thinking about how to pay your bills. When you are rich, you lay awake at night, wondering how your investments are doing; what friend, relative, or charity is going to hit you up for some money; or what the future of the stock market is. Who do you think sleeps better at night, Donald Trump or me?

Our culture has become astoundingly commercialized in order to get people to buy things. When I was growing up, television commercials took only two minutes out of every half hour. Now they take eight. When you go to a movie theater, subliminal advertising is intertwined with the movie to increase your desire for coke and candy. Schools are contracting with either Coke or Pepsi, but not both, as the only drink sold on campus. Billboards are everywhere. There is one situation that has moved me to take a stance. Companies have begun approaching school districts about contracting for the privilege of putting their company logos on school buses and buildings. We all know that school systems can use the money. As a member of the school board, how would you vote on this issue? How do you feel about corporate sponsorship for your school's athletic programs? It sure would help financially, but you've got to decide if corporate America is going to have its hand in everything. I want you to go one step further in your thinking. Should churches cater to corporations by allowing them to advertise in church books and publications? Lord knows the smaller churches can use the money. I am hopeful that as a society, we can become committed to the proposition that money will not be the ultimate decision maker on everything. We've got to make more of our decisions the old fashioned way with principles, commitment, and compassion.

I remember when "Buy American" was a prominent slogan. Walmart led the way, declaring that all their products were American-made. Then they were exposed for selling sweatshop goods and had to drop their slogan. It seems that everything is made overseas these days. It's just the free enterprise system working the way it's supposed to. Wages are cheaper overseas. Even when you add on shipping costs, many foreign goods are still cheaper than American goods. I went to a store a few of years ago and bought some topsoil. On the plastic bag was written, "Made in America." Thank God we still produce our own dirt. When we start buying dirt over- seas, I think it's time to get the heck out!

Until the last century, each generation took the basics from the previous generation, made some slight modifications, and continued on in much the same manner. This lack of change—called stability—did not advance our society very far technologically but worked very well in moving from one generation to the next without a lot of confusion. There is an adage that has been in existence for many years. The adage states, "If it ain't broke, don't fix it." Show me a company that uses this philosophy today, and I'll show you a company that is either out of business or is headed that way. If you wait until something goes wrong before you act, your competitors will pass you by. We now have a new concept called "proactive." We no longer look at what is already happening to decide what to do; we try to anticipate the future to solve problems before they happen. This concept sounds great, but it incorporates two concepts that are proven stress-producers: change, and pushing people to work harder. This looks to me like another way to squeeze employees.

The whole marketing philosophy in this country has done a complete change over the past thirty years. It used to be that someone saw a demonstrated need for something and then tried to create an invention based on that need. When the product was proven successful, it was marketed. For example, someone would make a determination that there was a need for a mousetrap. Based on that information, people would try to invent and market a mousetrap. Today, it works the other way around. What happens now is that someone invents a product even though there has not been a demonstrated need for it and then tries to create demand via marketing techniques. Most of the half-hour infomercials are designed to do exactly this. Somebody creates an invention before a need has been determined. The infomercials then try to convince the viewing audience that they need the product. People buy lots of stuff they don't need and end up kicking themselves for being taken for a ride.

Making Decisions

I recall a time when decision-making was a totally different process than it is now. We used to make decisions based on common sense, tradition, family values, rules, routine, and deciding what was best for the group. It seems that those methods of decision-making have fallen by the wayside. So what do we use as standards for decision-making today? The most prevalent way is the bottom line—money. It is sickening to hear that a great idea is shot down just because the money isn't available. It just says to me that we have our priorities out of whack. When you look at the great architectural projects of the past, it makes you wonder if these kinds of monuments will continue to be built in the future. If the ancient Romans or Greeks had used today's standard (money), most of the great architectural marvels of their time would never have been built.

Another tragedy of our time is the lawyer factor. You think a situation through and arrive at a decision you feel really good about. When you make a decision, the last thing you have to do before implementing it is to run it through your "lawyer mind" or maybe even seek a lawyer's opinion. Before you can implement any plan, you have to look at things from a worst-case scenario. You must do this to determine what the chances are that something could go wrong and a lawsuit would ensue. Let me give you an example in which "lawyer thinking" outdid common sense. As a high school teacher, my school had fire and bomb-threat drills that caused us to evacuate the school. When there was a bomb threat, we would probably be outside for more than an hour. It just so happened that my classroom was the one closest to the school child care center (another concept which was not around in my student days). My students were responsible for evacuating the babies and toddlers. We took the babies and toddlers to the top of the hill behind the school with the students. The mothers would sometimes join us to take care of their babies. One such drill occurred on a cold day in February, and the wind was blowing hard. On the previous practice evacuation, I had driven my van to the top of the hill in order to get the toddlers and babies out of the cold. When I offered my services this second time, the director of the child care center said she could not use my van as shelter because she had gotten in trouble the last time. The school administration had filtered the situation through their lawyer minds, and common sense went by the wayside. The school administration was only thinking about the liability issue should something go wrong.

They weren't concerned with the toddlers' wellbeing on a cold winter's day. They were just concerned about the possibility of a lawsuit. It seemed absurd to me.

I have another situation that doesn't pass "the giggle test." There was a busy intersection in front of my school. One of the streets zigzags at the intersection, which compounded the problem. A number of accidents had occurred at this intersection. School officials recommended to the state transportation department that a stoplight be installed at the intersection. The department complied with the request, and a traffic engineer was dispatched to the location. He had a formula where accidents, injuries, and deaths each count as a certain number of points. When he had finished his evaluation, he tallied up the points and stated that we were one death short of qualifying for a stoplight. There were people who wanted to throw this guy into the intersection during rush hour to get the additional points we needed.

The computer has become a major source of decision-making. You put raw data into the computer, and out comes your decision. I have never seen any human needs entered into the computer to affect the outcome. No human emotions of any kind are a part of this decision-making process. It is imperative to temper any statistical data with human factors to ensure a good all-around decision, not just a good statistical decision. Insurance companies rate near the top in their reliance on computer decision-making. They make all of their decisions based on computer input and output.

I have argued many times with insurance companies about their faulty decision-making, but I have always lost. It's hard to understand why they think a certain factor should be an entering argument while ignoring other factors that seem more applicable. The insurance companies have become more sophisticated as the years go by, and now they enter things into their database that seem irrelevant and can only work in their favor. If you are fifty years old and are applying for life insurance or health insurance, the insurance companies will find ways for their computers to increase your rates. Part of your application form will likely ask if you have ever smoked. If you smoked for six months while you were in high school and have not smoked for thirty years, you will fall into a different rate table than non-smokers and will pay higher premiums for your honesty. They will probably put you in the same category as someone who has smoked two packs a day for the last thirty years. The insurance companies can make their computers say whatever they want them to. Yes and no answers oftentimes are not adequate for good decision-making. I recall filling out questionnaires that were composed entirely of yes or no answers. For a lot of answers, yes or no answers were woefully inadequate. I sat there, wondering what they could possibly do with some of my answers. It reminded me of a trial where the prosecuting attorney asks yes or no questions. When a witness tries to give a full answer, the prosecutor cuts him off and demands that he give a yes or no answer. Witnesses in a trial should be allowed to answer questions completely, regardless of how questions are posed. What are the prosecutors afraid of—that the truth might come out when they are trying to suppress it, or because it might thwart their effort to mislead people?

Money, lawyers, and computers are flawed methods for decision-making. What other method of decision-making will be suitable, particularly for school kids? I've got it! Let 's use no-tolerance policies. A no-tolerance policy is one where all decisions are effectively made in advance by creating a decision table that takes common sense out of the equation. If a decision needs to be made, all that is required is for one to consult the decision table and announce the decision. A decision table is a matrix designed to improve decision- making. The concept is that you enter the table with a student infraction and the table leads you to the appropriate penalty. This tool has become very popular in schools to help enforce discipline uniformly. The decision table insures that all students committing the same crime will be punished in the same manner. No-tolerance means that principals are bound by the table and are not allowed to deviate under any circumstances. Prior to implementation of the no-tolerance policy guidelines, one student would commit an infraction of school rules and receive a three-day suspension by the principal. Another student would commit the same offense and be given only lunch detention by the assistant principal. The no-tolerance policy has done a great job of combating this flaw by having both principals use the same decision table. However, the policy has gone further than its original intent. A principal can tell you exactly what penalty exists for nearly every infraction by looking at his decision table. Decisions made by the decision table are non-negotiable; there can be no break of protocol. It must be administrated as an absolute, stand-alone instrument. No common sense is allowed. This method of administrating punishment assumes that you are using a perfect instrument to make decisions.

No weapon in school seems like a cut-and-dried policy. Surely we can apply a no-tolerance policy here. Let me describe two situations that might change your mind. The first case involved a fifth grade student who had a plastic knife in his backpack. He was intending to use the knife to spread his peanut butter at lunch. The knife was discovered; and based on the no-tolerance policy, a plastic knife is a knife with no distinction. The no-tolerance policy was invoked and the student was suspended for two weeks by his principal, per the decision table. The school superintendent was eager to demonstrate the integrity of this plan and allowed the decision to stand. The school board wanted to show solidarity with the superintendent and the principal and so they allowed the suspension to ride. The ACLU got wind of this fiasco and put egg on the faces of the entire district administration. The student was back in school the next day. Apparently, the judge was not in favor of no-tolerance policies that do not yield to common sense. An overrule policy is essential for situations where a no- tolerance policy becomes ludicrous.

A second case involving a no-tolerance policy

concerned an honor student who had gone fishing over the weekend. He forgot to take his all-in-one fishing tool (leatherman) out of his pocket prior to coming to school on Monday. Security conducted a random shake- down on Monday and the fishing tool was discovered. According to the no-tolerance policy, a knife is a knife and so this student was suspended for twenty days, causing him to flunk all his classes. His grade-point average plummeted, and the student was so emotionally defeated that he dropped out of school and spiraled down. I don't know what ultimately happened to this student, but the no-tolerance policy had seemingly ruined his life. These two situations did not pass the common sense test and yet were allowed to stand because the no-tolerance policy did not grant any latitude to the person administrating the decision table. I don't understand how somebody can better judge a situation before it happens than by obtaining the facts at the time of the event.

I guess no-tolerance policies are kind of like a preemptive military strike. If your enemies know that you are capable of a pre-emptive strike, they will be less inclined to do anything that would cause you to act first. In other words, the enemy knows in advance of commit- ting an offense what their punishment will be. As for students, if you put a strong policy in place that has no exclusions, students will be less likely to commit a pre-defined offense because they know in advance what the penalty will be. This kind of policy is similar to having the death penalty in our judicial system. Part of the idea behind the death penalty is to make people less inclined to commit a crime if they know the death penalty will be imposed. It hasn't deterred a single person from commit- ting a crime. I'm still waiting for the first set of studies to be published about schools using no-tolerance policies to see if these policies of predetermined punishments have really had some positive impact on student discipline.

Let's appoint ourselves as policy makers. We have to absorb the following information and establish some kind of policy. Some people want the speed limit to be 90 MPH. We can't do that because there would be too many deaths on the highway. If we are so concerned about people being killed on the highway, let's decide to make the speed limit 10 MPH. No one would get killed at that speed. This would be great for cutting down highway deaths, but nobody would get anywhere. At a speed limit of 10 MPH, the automobile industry would take a giant hit, as the industry's financial survival is predicated on accidents and stolen vehicles to create additional demand for cars. Eliminate accidents and stolen vehicles, and the auto industry would be crushed. If we all drove 10 MPH, nobody would get killed except the auto manufacturers.

I think you are all familiar with the reverse angle in sports. On football replays, they show the play from several angles to aid in making the correct call. A golfer will line up his putt from several angles to get his best read. I just wonder if our society could do a better job of making decisions using the reverse angle. One way to obtain several angles to aid in decision-making is by employing group decision-making. Each person in the group presents a different angle, making for better decisions. Our varying knowledge and experience define why group decision making is usually better than individual decision-making. I just told you that group decisions are usually better than individual decisions. Before you swallow the hook, take a look at some statements related to group decision-making:

1. "Two heads are better than one." To me, this infers that three heads are better than two and four heads are better than three.
2. "Too many cooks spoil the stew."
3. "Too many chiefs and not enough Indians." (You can't say this anymore as it is not politically correct).
4. "A camel is a horse by committee."

So what do these collective statements say? If I com- bine all the statements and temper it with some of my own experience and knowledge, I would say that groups can certainly come up with better decisions than individuals; however, if you get too large of a group, the decision-making suffers. Apparently, the best size for a group is around three to five people.

When you see the president conducting a meeting with his advisors, how many people are around the table? My guess is about fourteen. I sometimes wonder how they ever arrive at a decision they can all live with. The decisions of the biggest egos at the table will almost always win out over better decisions that come from weaker egos. How would a group proceed if everybody was equal in status and intelligence? It seems to me that this combination of group members would struggle the most. By the time everybody projected their prowess, the joint decision might not be any better than if they had a series of coin tosses at the outset of the meeting.

We almost completely ignore a method of decision-making that has been in place for hundreds of years and is woven into our Constitution. The method of decision- making I am referring to is called "the majority rules." You try to educate people as best you can about a subject and then put it up for a vote. The majority rules and the outcome is accepted as the group decision. This type of decision-making seems to be on the decline. Lawyers get in the way. Special interest groups get in the way. Political correctness gets in the way. The environmentalists and the ecologists get in the way. Poor losers tie up decisions in the courts for years. It's a mess. I always thought that a democracy was founded on having the majority rule. You can never make everybody happy, so let's make the greatest number of people happy by let- ting the majority rule.

I recall the commander of the Strategic Air Command (SAC), a four-star general who came to my squadron to exchange information with the troops in the field. He told us that he was always looking for better ways to do things. He stated that those of us doing the flying and fighting often had better ideas than the generals sitting behind their desks. He strongly encouraged us to send up to headquarters any suggestions we might have. He qualified his statement by telling us that there was no such thing as a bad suggestion. He also said that he would con- sider any suggestion as long as it wasn't illegal or immoral and that he would waiver immoral, if necessary.

After I had been in the Air Force for a while, I came to understand that promotions drive everything. High-ranking officers that were brilliant at saving money were passed over for promotion in favor of big spenders who demonstrated their clout by acquiring and spending unnecessary funds. Officers that know how to "pull strings" to get extra money from HQ or the Pentagon are always looked at as go-getters and worthy of promotion.

I was once stationed at a base that had Bermuda grass. Bermuda grass goes dormant in the winter and turns completely brown. When a general or congressman visit a base, there is always a maximum effort to spruce up the base to impress them. A typical base will spend about $25,000 on this endeavor. On one particular visit, the base commander wanted to impress the general by rolling out the red carpet; however, there was one major hurdle. The base didn't own any red carpet. The base commander was desperate to impress the general and so he ordered the paint shop to paint a red carpet on the tarmac. While he had the paint shop on the hook, the base commander told them to paint the grass green as well. If a congressman was scheduled to visit, it got even more ridiculous. This is the sort of thing high-ranking officers do if they are serious about getting promoted.

The military services are known to be very punitive compared to civilian life. The thought of a court- martial always loomed big in our minds. I saw people court-martialed for things that wouldn't even be considered as a wrongdoing in the civilian sector. A co-pilot in my squadron was court-martialed for having an honest, legitimate relationship with an enlisted woman. His career was over, and he had a "scarlet letter" that would show up on his FBI background investigation for the rest of his life. I also knew a young airman who was not good at managing his money. Nobody ever showed him how to do this. His mother was always bailing him out in order to keep his record clean. Finally, he ran into a situation where his mother put her foot down and told him that she would no longer bail him out. The Air Force got wind of his financial situation and he was court-martialed for bouncing a number of checks. He was given jail time and received a bad conduct discharge, something that will stay with him for the rest of his life. In civilian life, your career could never be ruined for committing these offenses. In fact, these two incidents would be "no counters," and an employer could get into trouble for investigating these individuals as these offenses are not work related. Sometimes you can't enact your best decision because of extenuating circumstances. A general rule in the business world is when a competitor makes mistakes, you stand your ground and watch them seal their own doom. However, there is one situation I came across that defies this kind of thinking. I heard the owner of a professional baseball team state that his was the only business in America where he was forced to match his competitors' dumbest mistakes. When the owners of other teams signed players to ridiculous contracts, he had to match them or he would not be competitive. Thus, he could go out of business for not matching his competitors' dumbest mistakes.

Another situation that defies routine decision-making is school transportation. I recently talked to a person who had worked for thirty-five years in the school transportation business and was currently working as a school transportation consultant. I asked him what he thought about school buses going high tech with alternative fuels and hybrid buses. He explained to me that government entities should not respond to competition the same way private companies do. Government entities should not try to be on the leading edge of technology. Their best move is to be on the trailing edge of technology. By being on the trailing edge of technology, schools can make their purchases after most of the bugs will have been worked out and new competitors have driven the prices down. This consultant thought that school transportation departments were better off not buying high-tech buses at this time. The trouble is that you are considered to be ineffective on your job if you can't lead your company into the future by acquiring leading-edge products. Transportation directors will appear to be regressive unless they prove that they are in touch with the trends in their area of expertise. Everybody wants to be on the leading edge of technology, but sometimes it is the wrong decision. You have to check things out from all angles and be prepared to buck the trend if that is the best decision for you. Remember, the government is different than most companies. They don't have to respond to the competition in the same way that corporate America does. A general rule is for government managers to avoid keeping up with the latest and greatest products until they have been around for a while. Wait until you are on the trailing edge of technology, and then make your move.

Perfection is the standard in many aspects of our lives. We expect perfection from the gadgets we buy. A microwave oven that works nearly all the time is not good enough. It is much the same with other things. When perfection is the goal, we can never exceed our goal and will usually fall short and create our own unhappiness. We tell people to "shoot for the stars." Obviously, if we set goals beyond our reach, we will induce failure and defeatism. People hate to miss a goal by just a little bit. As soon as a person perceives that he cannot attain his goal, he will quit on it. When he quits on it, he makes sure that he misses by a mile, not just an inch. It's easier on the human psyche that way. There are all kinds of success stories about people who hung in there and per- severed. Abraham Lincoln is a great example. He failed miserably at so many things that he should have given up a long time before he became president, but he hung in there and succeeded. The trouble with this scenario is that not everybody is Abraham Lincoln. He was a rare type of individual. Not everybody is cut out to hang in there forever. Just like not all people can become professional athletes or scientists, not all people have the talent to overcome immense obstacles. Some people are just not cut out to "get to the mountaintop." It is very important that we set our goals appropriately. If we set our goals too high, we set ourselves up for failure. If we set our goals too low, we will be mired in mediocrity. I remember a saying, "Show me a good loser, and I'll show you a loser." Winning is not just important to Americans; it's an obsession. Setting appropriate goals is extremely important to being satisfied with your accomplishments. This is why I am so dead set against concepts like "doing more with less." If you go through enough rounds of "doing more with less," eventually, you will be "doing everything with nothing." This type of mentality has all the potential to create failures among people who are less gifted than others.

Sometimes it's important to recognize failure for what it is and go in a different direction. This is what I did when I abandoned accounting in favor of the Air Force. If I had hung in there to prove that I could make it in accounting, I would have become a basket case. It's hard to figure out what to do sometimes. Go with your gut feeling, your instincts. They are the best barometers you have.

The question about putting all the military services

together has been raised several times. Even if all the services were combined, it doesn't mean than they would do anything different than they are doing now. It does not mean that all the services would begin to dress alike or take on each other's traditions. It mostly means that the services would begin to think as one, combine their thinking on procurement decisions, become more seam- less on combat operations, and have standardized terminology, weapons, and administration. A combined military service would become more cohesive, reduce waste, and create standardization among the services. All the services would use the same equipment in situations where it is feasible. It seems that this action would save a lot of money by cutting down on redundancy.

The first time the joint service concept was considered was in 1946 but the navy would not budge, and so the proposal was torpedoed. In 2006, there was a push to create a joint service medical organization but the concept was not able to gain traction. Recently, the various services made an effort to create a joint fighter airplane. The concept is that it is cheaper to develop one aircraft that satisfies the needs of all the branches of the military instead of each service developing its own aircraft. If this venture is successful, you will probably see more joint service weapons being developed and more money being saved. This action would be one small step toward combining the efforts of the military services which would cut costs and improve coordination among the services. Combining the military services would not eliminate the services as we now know them.

The services would simply look for areas where they can work in harmony before the war. They could combine their efforts in areas like administration, procurement, and terminology in order to improve cohesiveness and cut redundancy. A significant move in this direction is already in progress but military traditionalists will remain a constant obstacle to further progress.

So how has this joint service aircraft come out? The four services couldn't even agree whether the new fighter should have one engine or two. They couldn't agree on whether this new fighter should have one crew member or two. I don't understand the disagreement about whether the new fighter should have one engine or two. The F-16 has the nickname "disposable fighter." When you have two engines and you lose one, how many engines do you have left? The answer is one. If you have one engine on an airplane and you lose an engine, how many engines do you have left? The answer is zero. The F-16 has only one engine; hence, the nickname "disposable fighter."

There was indecision about whether the new fighter should have vertical takeoff capability. There were a host of other design characteristics that had to be resolved to everyone's satisfaction. There were a lot of disagreements in trying to arrive at a prototype that all the services could be happy with. Maybe the joint aspect of new aircraft can only go so far and then each service has to take it from there. We'll see.

I want to give you some information that you probably haven't thought about. The secretaries of all the military services (secretary of the army for example) are civilians; the secretary of defense is a civilian; the commander-in-chief is a civilian. There is a distinct reason why these positions are all designated for civilians. People in the military are taught to take that hill, bomb people into submission, and kill or be killed. When people enlist in the military, there is an indoctrination process called boot camp. This indoctrination is a fantastic tool for transforming civilians into sharp, team-oriented, well-disciplined fighting machines that have the mind- set that losing is not an option. Much of this transformation is imbedded for life. This metamorphosis that military members go through is why we have civilians in the top military positions.

In October 1962, the Cuban Missile Crisis led us to the brink of a nuclear war. When President Kennedy polled his staff about what we should do, General Curtis Lemay, the top spokesman for the people in uniform, wanted to invade Cuba. Thank God there were enough civilians in the room to push that thought away. I use this example to help you to understand what the military mindset has always been. Recently, General Petraeus took on the leadership role in Afghanistan. He did a great job, but I'm sure that he had to double think every- thing. His first instinct has to be that of a fighting man who wants to take it to the enemy in a big way. After he processes that thought, he has to temper his military thinking with some diplomacy, tact, and cultural under- standing. I don't think General Lemay had that capability in 1962.

There are new laws and rules established every day without many laws being repealed. This means that the number of laws on the books is climbing. I'm not implying that Gestapo tactics are making a comeback, nor am I comparing my country's freedoms with those of other countries. I just want to get a handle on which direction our freedoms are going. I want to compare our freedoms today with those of thirty years ago. The way things are headed, I can envision the day when all newborn babies will have a computer chip implanted where bone growth will eventually entomb it. The sup- porters of this procedure will say that it will make finding lost or abducted children easier. It will also be a great aid for catching criminals. It seems plausible that there would be a major showdown on this issue at some point. If this implanted computer chip were to become law, our civil rights are in serious trouble. It seems that the more technology advances, the greater the infringements on our freedoms become.

I want to use motorcycle helmet usage to demonstrate the difference between freedom and restricted freedom. Helmet usage for motorcycle riders has proven to substantially cut down on injuries and deaths. Even with this knowledge, there are still only twenty-one states that have adopted mandatory motorcycle helmet laws. These other states do not dictate that you can't wear a helmet. They are just leaving the decision up to you. They are giving you the right to exercise your freedom of choice. The question is, can we trust individuals to make good decisions, or do we need to employ lawmakers to make decisions for us? A lot of people say we can't afford to leave these kinds of decisions up to individuals because they routinely make poor choices. I guess that leaves us with having to rely on "big brother" to make decisions for us. If this is how you feel, your intentions are good but you are taking away individual freedom. The lack of a helmet law creates freedom of choice, which is a pillar in our Constitution. Some people I have talked to say that we do too much legislating and not enough educating. Legislating hinders your freedoms while educating preserves your freedoms. The problem with educating is that there are too many people who refuse to be educated and effectively misuse the freedoms given to them. This is why legislation happens more often than we wish it would.

Many motorcycle riders, given the option, will decide against wearing a helmet. There is more to this decision than the obvious. Motorcyclists who wear helmets survive accidents better than motorcyclists who do not wear helmets. However, motorcyclists who wear helmets will have more accidents because helmets hinder a rider's vision and hearing. What it boils down to is are you willing to have more accidents (due to vision and hearing restrictions) but have a higher survival rate because you are wearing a helmet; or would you rather have a lower crash rate (no restrictions on vision and hearing) but fare worse in crashes because you are not wearing a helmet? Maybe this scenario is the reason why a majority of the states are leaving the helmet choice up to the individual.

I feel that the motorcycle helmet issue can be expanded to explain disagreements on a large number of issues. When I watch the political commentators, there is always a common theme. That recurring theme is that there is too much government. The federal government has its hand in everything. The government is trying to tell fast food restaurants what they should have on their menus. The government is telling schools to eliminate junk food even though junk food is a money-maker for the schools. The government is trying to tell local communities how to teach sexual education. The list goes on and on. Do you recall when I explained the difference between theory and the application of theory? These issues I am describing are the absolute epitome of what I was describing. The theory is that there is no need for government interference in these issues because they are issues for individual people to resolve. People should be able take responsibility for these issues without government interference. The application of theory is when people take on these responsibilities. If people act responsibly, the government can stay away and everything works out great. The problem is that many people are not responsible enough to carry out their responsibilities. This leaves us with two possible solutions. We can just forget about the problems and let them continue to fester and grow, or have the government step in and take responsibility for the problems. This dilemma is not created by the government. If all people would act responsibly, the problem of government intrusion may well go away. It is up to the people to make the first move and then see if the government responds accordingly.

Parents that are 75 pounds overweight are not going to be responsible enough to manage their children's lives so that their children receive proper nutrition. When the citizens of the U.S. are not responsible, then the government feels the need to step in and manage their citizens. Unless the people of this country are willing to become more responsible, the government will always feel a need to tell people how to live their lives.

Children

Children—the future of our country. Much is said about our children, too much of which is negative. People insist, that children lack proper respect these days. People are (falsely) under the impression that teenagers are getting involved in crime more than previous generations did. This is a misconception conjured up by stories in the news. With a few exceptions, there are no bad children, just poor parenting skills. If you are not thrilled with the way today's teenagers have turned out, the blame has to go to the parents. Children are merely products of the world that we lay out for them.

I revel when I hear parents say to their children, "Act your age." What they really mean is, "Stop acting your age." Usually a child is acting appropriately for their age but the parents can't stand it. Parents, you need to wake up and learn to love and respect your children. If you had done this from your child's birth, you wouldn't be experiencing the relationship problems with your children that you are now. It seems that we have an entire generation of parents who had to be, "fashionable" or, "it just seemed natural" or, "they wanted to make their own parents proud by presenting them with grandchildren." Given the choice of bonding with their children or letting some form of entertainment substitute for bonding, too many parents find entertainment more fulfilling than spending time with their children.

Children really want discipline, boundaries, and limitations, even though they put up resistance when you try to instill them. My insight tells me that adults really want and need discipline, boundaries, and limitations, too. Who is there to monitor and enforce these kinds of things for adults? The more freedom we have in our society, the less ability we have to set boundaries and limitations on people. Morals don't seem to get the job done anymore. As adults we are expected to police ourselves. We don't need anyone setting boundaries and limitations on us. We're grown ups, not children. So how do we protect *us* from *ourselves?* That's a good question because I see a great number of adults who need to be protected from themselves. Apparently, there is an assumption that all adults are qualified to manage their lives without outside interference (unless they decide to seek it on their own.) It seems that those who need help the most are the ones who seek it the least. How do we solve that problem in a democracy? I know! You hear it all the time—education, education,

education, and then these people will figure it out for themselves. This does not work.

When I was a teenager, the statement, "Because I said so" was enough rationale to induce correct behavior on my part. That doesn't seem to work anymore. American children no longer react appropriately to this. However, I think our children have a valid point on this one. A parent should be able to come up with a better rationale than, "Because I said so." As a parent, you need to think the situation through well enough to determine a better rationale than, "Because I said so." If you can't come up with a better reason, you need to determine why you made the statement. Do you really have a good reason, or are you saying it just because your parents said it to you. I always try to give a rationale to my teenagers as to why they should behave in a certain manner. Quite often this is very tough to do. A statement from me such as, "Because having pride is important" just doesn't get the job done.

So now I've just taken away one of your prime weapons in dealing with your children. You can no longer get away with the statement, "Because I said so." Hang on. I am not going to give your children the upper hand so easily. I have a technique to substitute for the one I just took away. It is called, "Make a statement; ask a question." Instead of yelling at your child to clean her room, try substituting a, "Make a statement; ask a question" method of relating. The first thing you do is make a statement, "Your room is a mess." Then ask a question, "What do you intend to do about it?" If you have used an appropriate tone of voice, a child will usually respond in a positive way and give you and answer you can both live with. Remember, you have veto power if the child comes up with an unsatisfactory response. You can let her know that her plan is not acceptable and ask her to come up with another plan-of-action. Let's say you really wanted your child to start cleaning her room immediately. Unfortunately, her plan is to clean it up before she goes to bed. At this point, you are going to have to evaluate your child's plan to determine if it is valid. You want the room picked up right now; but is there any reason why it has to be that way, or are you just pulling a power play on your child? It's kind of like the, "Because I said so" analogy. You have to check yourself to see if you have a valid reason for wanting the room cleaned now. The beauty of this scenario is this: You don't have to constantly monitor your child to see if she is living up to her word. At the time you make the agreement with your child about the details of the chore, you also define a consequence to be executed should your child not live up to the terms that she came up with. your child is not likely to violate her own rules-of-engagement in this type of scenario. Since your child set up the terms, she likely will abide by them. Therefore, don't spend all day monitoring to see if your child is going to fulfill her duties. Simply wait until the next morning. If the room has not been cleaned as agreed upon, simply impulse the pre-announced penalty. At this point, tell her this chore must be done immediately or a second penalty will be imposed. One of the important factors in the entire agreement is that you be very specific about what you expect of your child. If cleaning her room includes dusting, make sure to say this specifically. Put it in writing if you must, and have both parties sign it. If part of cleaning up her room is to put all her dirty clothes in the hamper, say so very specifically. This is one area where my children got the best of me until I learned to be specific. When I announced to my children, "Go clean your room," it took a few knock down, drag-outs before I was able to fine-tune my approach. Don't let your children get away with technicalities. They are just testing you. Stand up and be the parent. By using this style of parenting, I guarantee an improved relationship with your child. You can determine for yourself which kinds of penalties work best for you. The ones I use on my teenagers are no telephone, no TV, no computer, and no friends. These consequences seem to work well for me.

The beauty of this kind of interaction with your child is that there is no parent-child confrontation. Your child does not feel she is being forced into doing things on her parent's terms. There is no power struggle, yet what needs to get done, gets done. The children of today are taught to think for themselves more than I was. Kids today are taught to think their way out of situations. This is helpful in situations such as child abuse or abduction. There are times where this line of thinking can work against us. Use the "Make a statement; ask a question" style of parenting as necessary to help you maintain control of your children who try to think their way out of things.

As a child, I remember getting into all kinds of irritating situations involving food. Like all children, I did not always like the food put on my plate. In those days, much more than today, children were told to eat their food because children were starving in India or Africa. I never could see how eating my beets was going to help starving children on the other side of the world. I told my parents to ship the lousy food to the starving countries. This would make everybody happy. What I came up with when I was a little older was the "Pipeline to India." I would pretend that the garbage disposal was the "Pipeline to India" and send my unwanted food to them.

There is another aspect of parenting which is parallel to the way military people interpret regulations. In the military there are those who say you can't do something unless the regulations say you can; and there are those who say you can do something unless the regulations specifically state that you can't. I think some parents are in the mode of saying "No" unless there is a compelling reason to say, "Yes." Other parents say, "Yes" unless there is a compelling reason to say, "No." Which kind of parent are you? Often times the "No" parent is the overprotective parent who fosters insecurity or rebellion in her children. Be careful about saying "No" when you have no justification for it.

I'm surprised that America's children aren't more confused than they are. Grandma tells them to play by one set of rules; Mom tells them to play by a different set of rules; Dad tells them to play by a third set of rules; and schools tell them to play by yet another set of rules. School all by itself is a tough place to abide by the rules. I watched a documentary in which school discipline was compared with discipline methods used by prisons. It was amazing how comparable the two institutions were. The number of security cameras used in schools rivaled the number used in prisons. The schools had uniformed guards just like the prisons did. The way the students were spoken to by teachers and staff was probably worse than the way prison staff spoke to the prisoners.

I recently chaperoned some fifth grade students on a field trip. I couldn't believe how mollycoddled the students were. Everything the teachers said to the students was in a very nice tone of voice (too nice for me). However, it seemed that everything said to the students was put to them as a threat or a reward scenario. Also, the number of directions given to the students was enormous. They were coached on everything to the point that the students did not have to think for themselves. They knew that one of the three teachers would do their thinking for them and offer a reward/punishment scenario.

Systemic Problems in Our Education System

When I worked as a high school teacher, I once made this statement to my principal: "If our school district were a business, it would have gone bankrupt years ago." In comparing the strides I have seen in education over the past thirty years with the strides I have seen in business or the Air Force, education is way behind. Putting computers in schools, utilizing block scheduling, and creating decisive standardized testing are not enough. Several people have explained to me why education is so slow to make changes. If you will recall, I am not big on theory, but I am very big on the application of theory. Educational theories leave a lot to be desired. One contemporary theory states that everything should be related to standardized test scores. School funding, teachers' pay, teacher hiring and firings, and an assortment of other functions would be tied to standardized test results. Along with the good that will happen, some negative consequences will evolve. Teachers will teach to the standardized tests instead of teaching material essential to a well-rounded education. With so much riding on these standardized tests, students and teachers feel more pressure than ever to achieve lofty goals. The four core courses (English, math, science, and social studies) will potentially flourish at the expense of elective courses that are not part of the equation for measuring school success, but are part of the equation for post-high-school success.

Schools requiring students to pass a graduation exam are raising their dropout rate as a bi-product. At the high school where I taught, half the students failed the graduation test on their first attempt. A large number of students who failed the exam dropped out of school rather than take the test for a second time. When seniors take the standardized tests, the tests prove to be an up or out scenario for many of them. I'm not sure the educational theorists realized that this might happen when they created the concept of a graduation exam. Their intentions were very good, as they thought the exit exams would encourage students to rise to the challenge and prove themselves. What has happened is that a lot of students are pulling up short of the goal line.

As we put more emphasis on the core courses by increasing their requirements to graduate, we are creating fewer opportunities for students to take elective courses. Elective courses afford students the opportunity to take courses that will shape their post-high-school decisions.

Education needs to make some radical changes. Everything should be on the table. Putting everything on the table means dismissing every practice, procedure, and theory currently in use and building a new system from the ground up. As you build your new system, you can add back the parts of the old system that worked well. The first problem that has to be solved before building a new education system is to understand why so many students aren't motivated to learn. You can develop a fantastic educational program, but if the students are not motivated to learn it, your efforts are diluted. Raising the bar motivates the students at the top but defeats the students at the bottom. Unmotivated students are ripe for becoming dropouts. Some students will eventually drop into prison if the education system can't hold onto them. Schools have to be more responsible for how their students end up in life. Students need to be more responsible for where they end up in life. It has to be a two-pronged attack. Elective courses have to be an integral part of the education plan.

School has always been deemed appropriate for ages five to eighteen. Maybe it's time we looked at what students really need to know and when do they need to know it. There is a lot more to the real world than math, science, English, and social studies. I would recommend that no one graduate from high school without learning about insurance, taxes, marriage relationships, parenting, buying and maintaining a car, renting or buying a house, and a host of other skills people need to know in order to make it in society. None of these elements can be found on a standardized test, so they are treated as being superfluous. How can we possibly emphasize only core courses and yet teach students the life skills they desperately need to learn? One answer might be to keep students in school for an extra year. Lots of children are not ready to face adult challenges at age eighteen. What if an extra year of school was designed for students to take electives to aid them in making better post-high- school decisions? An extra year of school would be expensive but paying for prison, welfare, and crime are also expensive.

Students today want to understand how classroom materials relate to their post-graduation lives before they can become genuinely interested. If the material is pure academics, many students won't care enough to learn it. When I compare this attitude to my generation, I see a huge difference. In my generation, we all wanted to learn the material in school just to please our parents. I don't recall being concerned with how the classroom material related to the real world. Teaching to the real world as well as the academic world will be a significant challenge for teachers. I can't understand why we have gravitated toward requiring all students to take four years of high school math. I suspect that the third and fourth years are significant factors in the dropout rate. Ninety percent of all students will work in jobs where two years of math will suffice. I was an accountant, an Air Force navigator, a high school teacher, and a college professor, and I never took the third or fourth years of math. Instead of math, I took electives. Very few jobs require calculus or trigonometry, so what is the point in having everybody study them? The third and fourth years of math should be optional. They need to be offered as elective courses for students who need to take them as college prerequisites. Making all students take four years of math is increasing the dropout rate needlessly. It would be much more beneficial for students to take elective courses than requiring them to take a fourth year of math. Elective courses are the engine by which many students find their niche. Elective courses in woodworking, bookkeeping, computers, office management, and child development are substantially more useful to most students than the last two years of math. I honestly think that a class in anger management would benefit students more than taking a fourth year of math.

We need to be more selective in determining what students really need to learn. States and state capitals have always been a staple in grade school. Complex math has always been a staple in high school. Maybe we need to rethink what students need to know. Do students really need to memorize the state capitals when they can look them up in a few minutes on the Internet? Do students need to know all the math concepts we now teach, or can we just let them use calculators? Granted, we need to have some people that know more than how to punch numbers into a calculator. Those students would be your third- and fourth-year math students. There are many methods we use to evaluate students' comprehension. Some of these methods are fill in the blank, multiple choice, essays, speeches, compare and contrast, and demonstrations. Which of these testing methods mirrors life itself? Do we only need to know things in life well enough to recognize the correct answer from a list of choices, or is life more like fill in the blank where we must be able to recall answers with nothing to prompt us. Schools need to give consideration to educating and evaluating students using methods that mirror life itself. Isn't that what we are trying to educate our children for—life?

Another idea that is extremely outdated is the grade level concept. Not all students learn at the same rate, yet we push them to the next level as groups, whether they are individually ready or not. No one should ever get promoted all the way to high school and not know how to read and write; but it happens all the time. I taught several high school students that could read at only a first-grade level. Every one of these students' prior teachers chose to promote them to the next grade knowing that they read at a first-grade level. This tragedy is a genuine disservice to both the students and their future teachers.

Reading is absolutely paramount to learning. If you can't read, you will be unable to learn in your other classes. With that as a backdrop, what would happen if reading and writing comprised eighty percent of the curriculum for the first two years of school? Students would not be allowed to advance to the next level until they prove that they can read at a satisfactory level. Once reading and writing are mastered, the students could move on to other subjects. The problem with this concept is that it interferes with the grade level concept. Some children will be ready to advance sooner than others, causing children of differing ages to be schooled together.

Let's take a look at the parameters of education, beginning with the top: the PhD. Our society puts a huge premium on post-secondary education. We encourage everybody to seek more education. It seems that a college degree now goes about as far a high school diploma did a couple of generations ago. If I project out for several decades, I see a society of 90 percent PhD's. This will not be a fun society to live in. I lived in Los Alamos, New Mexico for five years. Los Alamos has the highest concentration of PhD's in the world. It was a microcosm of what the rest of the country is trying to become. Because these PhD's are geniuses in their fields, they usually think they are smarter than other people that work in non-PhD fields. My wife was a pharma- cist and she told me about it all the time. These PhD's thought they knew more about pharmacy than she did. They might be able to use their brainpower to figure out what would work best for them, but they don't know the laws governing pharmacy, many of which do not inter- face well with scientific reasoning.

There are a number of eccentrics amongst these PhD's. I can see nothing but misery in a world comprised of all PhD's. Who would do the menial tasks in an all-PhD world? If I recall my economics correctly, the laws of supply and demand dictate that people doing the menial tasks would be commanding big salaries while the PhD's would be making peanuts. Having a PhD has always been a status symbol. With so many people get- ting PhD's today, it seems logical that a new degree (or two) above a PhD will soon be conspired. We will always have need for educationally elite people in our society.

Stay with me while we travel on the education train down from the PhD level to the GED level. The GED has been highly praised since its inception, but I see a number of concepts that could use some adjusting. I believe the GED was invented to serve adults in their twenties, thirties, and forties to give them a second chance at a high school diploma; however, it is currently being used by many students as an alternative to high school. It caused the dropout rate to increase significantly at the high school where I taught. I had students drop out of school during the fall semester of their junior year, and they would come back four months later to show me their GED certificate. Why should students stay in school if it is that easy to get a GED? When I compared a GED certificate with a regular high school diploma, I could not tell the difference, even after comparing them for quite a while. They looked identical to me. The GED graduate had to show me the difference. The regular diploma had the name of the high school on it while the GED certificate did not. Otherwise, the diplomas were identical. There is no way that any employer or recruiter is going to recognize the difference between the two.

I propose raising the GED entry level to age twenty- one. This would counteract the migration of students from high school to GED programs. GED programs should require students to apply the same effort as high school students. This would encourage more students to stay in school. Also, we need a public relations campaign to educate people on why a diploma is better than a GED. If a high school diploma really is no better than a GED, we are fighting a losing battle to keep our children in school.

Systemic educational problems need to be attacked at their root source. Education parallels life itself. First, you have to learn how to crawl, then walk, and then run. Lots of educational philosophy makes the assumption that we are at the "run stage." I would say that we are at the crawl stage on many issues. The crawl stage involves finding ways to increase students' motivation and enjoyment at school. If we don't fix these problems, the other problems will remain unresponsive. Improving students' attitudes is not going to be easy; however, I see very few people at the highest levels of educational reform giving much attention to this area. What would happen if we donated the first ten minutes of every class to doing nothing but having fun? My guess is that the students will learn more in the remaining fifty minutes than they now do in sixty minutes. Many of these students have terrible home lives. We will lose these children unless we attempt to motivate them by whatever means possible.

The Shuman Education Plan for Success

Here is my take on changing our education system in order to solve many problems inherent in today's educational system.

Virtually all teaching would be accomplished by computer tutorial. Tutorial lessons would be broken down into individual learning blocks. The concept of grade levels would be eliminated and would no longer be referenced. Doing away with grade levels allows each student to progress within her comfort zone. Students' progression will be measured solely by the number of tutorial blocks they have successfully completed. Let's say that the designers of the tutorial blocks decide that a student needs to complete five hundred blocks of instruction to signify high school graduation. Graduation would be awarded when students successfully complete all the learning blocks. Students that fall behind can be easily identified and targeted for teacher intervention.

Students would be assigned to a traditional reading class for approximately their first two years of school. This class would be taught by a reading teacher in con- junction with computer learning. Under no circumstances will students advance to the next phase of comprehensive tutorials until they have demonstrated proficiency in both reading and computer skills.

Another basic premise of this plan is that all schools would be attended by students of all ages. Individual classrooms would consist of students of all ages. This arrangement should knock down some barriers and create more of a family atmosphere in the classroom. With students of all ages in each class, older students can help the younger students, which will take a load off of the teacher. By using this system, there would be no stigma about which students are the most capable or least capable students in the class. Students would rapidly adapt to being around students of all ages. It is possible that students, particularly the younger ones, would demonstrate accelerated emotional progress by being around older students. I recommend having a circular table with partitions to accommodate four students of different ages. With students of different ages at each station, younger students can ask an older student sitting nearby for help with a problem. This would allow teachers to work with students whose needs for assistance are greater. The idea of putting high school students in the same class- room with third graders might be troublesome for some people. Remember, students do not change rooms during the day, so younger students and older students will never be in the hallway together. The only time younger and older students are together is in their own class- room. Lunch could be arranged so that students of the same age could eat together.

One day per week, students would abandon tutorial learning in favor of traditional classroom instruction. Students would be grouped by age for this one special day each week. For students age twelve and under, part of their traditional day would incorporate a session on character issues. People such as policemen, ex-prisoners, motivational speakers, people who have successfully emerged from poverty, and military members would make excellent guest speakers. Introductions to peer pressure, smoking, drinking, and drugs would be a part of character education for all ages. I recommend a forty-five-minute block of character education on this special day for younger students. For ages thirteen and older, their day of traditional instruction would include one hour each on character issues and life skills. I recommend that character education be accomplished much like the younger students, only for a longer period of time. The older students would also receive instruction on life skills. Life skills are things like banking, car insurance, income taxes, relationships, marriage, health insurance, investments, renting versus buying, etc. People working in life skills types of professions should be invited as guest speakers. Other types of things that would be useful on traditional days are exercises involving teamwork and individual brain teasers.

Another basic premise in this plan is that there would be forty-five minutes devoted each day to physical fitness activities. There should be some strength conditioning combined with aerobic activities and some fun, team-oriented games. The student tutorial computers should be set up so that students cannot open any block of instruction until they have passed a required test at the end of the previous block. If a student fails a block test, the computer will revert to the study phase for remedial learning. If a test is failed for the second time, a teacher must work with the student one-on-one until the student can pass the block test. This is what the real **No Child Left Behind** is all about. Since classes are composed of students of all ages, falling behind is not a social issue because nobody would know.

I feel that this method of teaching lets all students take advantage of the brightest minds we can hire to develop the blocks of instruction. Another basic premise is that the same tutorials would be used in all schools across the country. This would go a long way toward leveling the playing field for substandard schools. Also, if all schools throughout the country use the same tutorial system, student transfers across town or across the country would be completely seamless. Students could pick up at their new school exactly where they left off at their old school.

One problem that would have to be addressed is what to do with students who finish all the required blocks of instruction well ahead of the normal graduation point. One suggestion is for them to become one-on-one instructors for students who are struggling. These students are obviously very bright and could make good one-on-one instructors. A second suggestion is for these students to take college classes online.

Another problem we would have is grades. There would be no grades, only block completions. When all the blocks are successfully completed, the students will receive a high school diploma. There would need to be a way to get past resisters and pessimists who would balk at any system that does not require grades. Without grades, a problem is created on how students would qualify to get into college or apply for scholarships. Without grades, I think we would need to evaluate students' potential based on standardized test scores, recommendations, and interviews.

Another point of contention is that teachers, except the ones teaching reading classes, would have one area of specialization but would need to be well versed in all subjects. To ensure that teachers can adequately teach all subjects, they would have their own software to aid them in becoming proficient in all subjects. If teachers get bogged down on a particular subject area when working with a student, they could change classrooms with another teacher who is better versed in that subject. If the students saw this happening on a regular basis, they would think nothing of it. They would not interpret their teacher exchanging rooms as anything unusual. Teachers could take teacher tutorials during the summers to strengthen their weak areas. Another matter that would need to be examined is teacher-student ratios. If it is determined that a teacher using computer tutorials can successfully manage five more students than under the traditional system, that would create a substantial savings by reducing the number of teachers required. Part of this savings could be used to increase teachers' pay.

One theme that should be present is that learning by computer can be fun. I recommend incorporating occasional humor, games, or mind teasers in each block of instruction to keep the students stimulated. We might even consider having a few short blocks dedicated entirely to games, mind teasers, or humor. This new system of education addresses many of today's educational problems. Here is a summary of problems remedied by this new system of instruction:

1. The same education is provided at all schools, rich or poor, east or west.
2. There would be no "social graduation" where students are promoted to the next grade when they are not ready.
3. Character education and life skills will be pillars in this system and should produce better citizens upon graduation.
4. All students will acquire the necessary computer skills to prepare them for future employment.
5. It seems plausible that the dropout rate will decrease.

6. Student learning will be enhanced.
7. Transfer of students to different schools would be seam- less, as the new school would have the same learning blocks as the old school. The students can pick up exactly where they left off.
8. A strong physical fitness program will be resurrected.
9. Because of the life skills taught on a routine basis, students will have the skills to "graduate into the real world" instead of graduating into the "school of hard knocks."
10. Teacher and student stress levels will abate.
11. Students' confidence levels will increase, particularly among less talented students.
12. Teachers will not be burdened with creating daily lesson plans or tests.
13. Better qualified teachers will be easier to recruit if the potential teachers like the new system.
14. Cliques among students should be dampened because students interact with students of all ages. Classrooms should be more like families.
15. Students' morale should improve.
16. AIMS scores should increase (or they might become obsolete).
17. Recurring expenses for textbooks will go away.
18. Students never have to worry about what they missed while they were absent. They just pick up where they left off.

School buildings and transportation costs can be significantly reduced as a component of this education plan. Here are explanations of how the savings would be created.

Since all schools would have students of all ages, this should help avoid situations where some schools are underutilized while other schools are overcrowded. Utilizing each school effectively could allow school districts to avoid building new schools or they might be able to close existing schools.

With our current system, a high school student who lives across the street from an elementary school is bused to the high school. An elementary student who lives next to the high school is bused to the elementary school. This is wasteful. Under my education plan, neither of these students would be bused. All students would attend the school closest to their home. Many current bus riders would now walk to school. Millions of dollars in transportation expenses could be saved by implementing this innovative system.

Let me restate the potential savings for this new system of education. Savings will come from better usage of school buildings, less bus transportation, doing away with textbooks, and savings from having fewer teachers (only if revised student-teacher ratios seem reasonable). The main costs to implement this new system are those of computers, computer desks and partitions, and the creation of universal computer learning blocks. The future savings dwarf the investment costs required. The money expended to acquire computers and computer desks should be considered as an investment, not an expense. There will be a tremendous return on this investment.

In conjunction with this fundamental change in education, I highly recommend that all schools adapt to year-around education. When students return to school after long summer breaks, it takes six weeks of refresher learning to get the students back to where they were before the summer break. Year-around schooling means going to school the same number of days as a traditional schedule; it is just a different schedule that seems to have the advantages of traditional schedules but with less disadvantages. Year-around school means having little mini breaks throughout the year instead of having a long break in the summer. This system should help reduce stress for teachers and students alike. It also makes it easier to plan family vacations for parents that cannot take summer vacations.

I'm not certain the current educational leaders are up to the task of implementing a new educational system at this time. However, it will take ten years to develop this new system, and our educational system will be ready by then if we change our mindset beginning now. Let's be proactive and look over the horizon instead of simply stomping out brush fires. We have an educational crisis that will take ten years to fix. Let's get going!

Racism, Stereotyping, Discrimination, and Culture

The topics mentioned in the above title are very sensitive and no matter how I present my information, I will upset some people. I want for you to open your mind, take a neutral stance, and apply some real common sense.

It is interesting, and sometimes maddening, how civil rights (individual rights) have evolved over the past fifty years. When I think about what civil rights laws were designed for, I think about laws designed to assist people to refute exclusion and promote inclusion. With the support of civil rights laws, people on the outside looking in are able to become insiders. Today, there are segments of our society that invoke their civil rights in the opposite way to propel themselves away from inclusion and into exclusion. These people want to be segregated from society's mainstream and readily use the courts and the ACLU to assist them in attaining exclusion.

Okay, Shuman, what do you mean when you say that people invoke their civil rights to gain exclusion from the mainstream on particular issues? I have an example to enlighten you. An upheaval occurred recently about high school yearbook pictures. Boys were supposed to wear tuxedos, and girls were supposed to wear drapes. A lesbian announced that she wanted to wear a tuxedo for her picture. The idea of one person imposing her will on so many people seems incredibly selfish. This girl needs to find another way to express her civil rights without directly impeding the legitimate happiness of so many people. The million dollar question is how far does one go to make themselves happy when they know that their actions are making other people unhappy? It is commonplace anymore for the courts to side with the non- conformists to protect their rights over the happiness of the conformists. My problem is not with the courts; it is with anybody that makes themselves happy at the expense of other people.

Time and again you see where people value themselves above a group that is asking for their cooperation. What if some of the boys had their pictures taken in McDonald's work outfits? It is obviously within their rights. Having non-conformists in a group setting causes the group to fracture. Whatever happened to teamwork? Doing what is asked of you is being part of the team. Our society has moved in the direction of valuing individual rights above teamwork, unity, cohesiveness, and inclusion. It's like a game where non-conformists are saying, "You can't make me." When a group becomes strongly unified and one person decides to stand up to them, it creates friction, much of which is needless. There are exceptions, of course.

It seems that the courts understand individual rights but are numb to group rights. The authors of our Constitution understood the value of preserving individual rights and spelled them out convincingly. However, the Constitution doesn't speak specifically about group rights in the same way. Is this an oversight to the Constitution? Are group rights inherent to the point that nothing needs to be said? It seems to me that individual rights are trumping group rights at an accelerating rate.

Group rights are just an accumulation of individual rights. Individuals should not make hundreds of people unhappy to promote their ideologies or agenda. This yearbook picture incident goes against several of **my basic principles**: (1) Your rights stop where my rights start. The smoking issue defines this principle very well. You can exercise your rights until you start impeding on my rights. Then you have to stop; (2) Make the greatest number of people happy by letting the majority rule; (3) You can't always get your way, so you must learn to adjust; (4) When in Rome, do as the Romans do. Individual rights need to work in harmony with group rights.

Now it's on to racism. I want to separate racism

into two basic components. The first component is real racism, racism that blatantly exists. Real racism involves deliberate acts of malice directed at a person(s) with race being the primary motive for the person's actions. As a society, we have made many strides forward on real racism. When you compare today's society with the one that required blacks to ride in the back of the bus or to use separate bathrooms or restaurants than whites, we have made great progress but still have a ways to go. There is a second component of racism that might never be resolved. This second component is perceived racism. What I mean by perceived racism is racism that exists only in our minds and is not real. Some people are predisposed or hyper-sensitized to see racism where it does not exist.

Let me cite an example where racism is nearly always perceived but does not necessarily exist. You are driving down the street and see a black person fighting another black person. You don't give it a second thought. You keep driving and you see a white person fighting another white person. You don't give it a second thought. Now you come across a situation where a black person is fighting a white person. Your instincts tell you that race is a factor. You think this even though this fight is for the same reasons as the other two fights. If you do this, you are perceiving racism when it does not necessarily exist.

I see black political commentators on TV that seem to see racism in every possible situation. They think they are doing blacks a favor by standing up for them but often times they are doing just the opposite. When they falsely cry racism, they are turning off whites to race issues. The white mentality becomes, "Well they're going to cry racism no matter what we do, so why even try."

Racism is a two-way street. Whites are victimized by blacks in the same manner that blacks are victimized by whites; however, you almost never hear a white person declare publicly that he was a victim of racism. I see a couple of possible explanations why this might be so. It is along the same lines as husbands' unwillingness to publicly state that they have been abused by their wives or girlfriends. Husbands who publicly accuse their wives of physical abuse are often ridiculed by insensitive or naïve people. These husbands often wish they had never said anything about what happened. A second reason you rarely hear whites allege racism against blacks deals with atonement. Most whites understand that their forefathers disparaged blacks. Subconsciously, they feel that they owe restitution to the current generation of blacks. This feeling makes whites less likely than blacks to proclaim racism in an equivalent situation.

White people are under-sensitized to race issues while black people are over-sensitized to race issues. Until this gap in sensitivity can be closed, there will always be race problems. The differences in life experiences between blacks and whites will always create perceived racism. Blacks are highly sensitized to racial prejudice, discrimination, and bigotry. Many blacks, particularly the poorer ones, have encountered a steady diet of race propaganda during their entire lives. Depictions of blacks being beaten and killed in the 1950s and KKK members yelling, "white power," have caused blacks to become hyper- sensitized to race issues—and understandably so. These experiences cause blacks to see racism in many situations where race is not the issue. President Obama recently addressed a joint session of Congress to lay out his plan for healthcare. A congressman lost his cool and shouted liar at President Obama. Unbelievably, there were some blacks that cited racism as the motive for the congress- man's outburst. To cite racism in this situation ruins these blacks credibility. Blacks are hurting their cause when they cite racism too easily, particularly when race proves not to be a factor after all the evidence is in. If all acts of real racism were permanently eliminated, perceived racism alone would perpetuate racial problems. Perceived racism is just as damaging to race relations as real racism. To make real progress in race relations, two things must happen. Blacks must withhold their declarations of racism until there is more evidence than the fact that a black person was victimized by a white person. What appears to be racism at first glance might not be racism at all. Blacks need to understand that they do not lose their opportunity to cite racism just because they don't make an immediate assertion. One can still claim racism after all the facts are in; a proclamation at that point will be more credible. The recommendation that I have for whites is to recognize the sensitivity blacks have about race issues and to avoid practicing real racism and the appearance of racism. What I mean by avoiding the appearance of racism is to apply the same standards to racial conduct that are now applied to sexual harassment cases. In sexual harassment cases, the view of the accused person is largely ignored in favor of the victim's view- point. If the victim thinks that she was harassed, then she was. The intention of the accused person is not the measuring stick for determining sexual harassment; the opinion of the victim is the determining factor. Some courts have ruled that men and women, as a general rule, have different levels of sensitivity. Conduct that does not offend most reasonable men might offend most reasonable women. In one study, two-thirds of the men surveyed said they would be flattered by a sexual approach in the workplace, while 15 percent would be insulted. The figures were reversed for women responding. Differing levels of sensitivity have led some courts to adopt a "reasonable woman" standard for judging cases of sexual harassment. Under this standard, if a reasonable woman would feel harassed, harassment may have occurred even if a reasonable man might not see it that way. Because the legal boundaries are so poorly marked, the best course of action would be to avoid all sexually charged conduct in the workplace. You should be aware that your conduct might be offensive to a co-worker and govern your behavior accordingly. Hypersensitivity is a major factor in how people perceive racism. Hypersensitivity is derived from our life experiences, particularly bad ones, and puts blinders on us. It predisposes us to make judgments that favor our sensitivities over reality. When two people are given the same information, a person who is hyper-sensitized to the information will see things differently than the other person. White people need to apply this same line of reasoning to their racial thinking. They need to avoid doing things that could be interpreted by some blacks as racism. Can you recall a situation where a word created an entirely different image in your mind than it did for other people? Hyper-sensitization causes this to happen. When I was in the Air Force, I was sensitized to flying, uniforms, customs and courtesies, etc. When someone said the word chow, it meant food to me; it meant the chow hall. For someone else, chow might mean a dog. For a third person, the word chow might relate to China. This is how hyper-sensitization works. When the word castle is introduced, one person might think of a game of chess. Another person might think of a fortress in England with a moat and a drawbridge. The thing that comes to my mind is Castle AFB. How you perceive racial issues is based on how sensitized you are to situations that have occurred in your life. Bill Cosby and former President Carter went on record to say that there are white people that would never vote for a black person. This is a true statement as far as they went, but they elected to ignore additional facts that would undermine their rationale. The percentage of blacks that would never vote for a white (over a black) is much higher than the percentage of whites that would never vote for a black (over a white). Part of the dynamics of this situation is the Uncle Tom effect in which blacks feel a need to stick together or become an outcast in their community. In the 2008 presidential election, 95 percent of blacks voted for Obama. This is the part that Bill Cosby and President Carter did not address. They preferred to use selective memory and hoped that it would stick. A first step in reducing perceived racism and better identifying real racism is to establish some ground rules to aid in forming a solid basis for determination. Let's start out with situations that involve the police since these cases are always high profile and can greatly influence people's opinions. Before a person is allowed to claim racism against a police officer, he would have to abide by two rules: (1) he must comply with all of the policeman's instructions; if the officer says to get out of your house or car, you need to get out of your house or car; if the officer says to get on the ground, you must get on the ground; (2) the suspect must refrain from becoming belligerent at the officer. If both of these rules are followed, racism perpetrated by the officer will become much clearer. This rule works well for both the officer and the offended person. Once either of these two rules is broken, the right to claim racism will be forfeited. Even if you lose your right to claim racism, you still retain your right to declare police brutality or police misconduct. You never lose these rights.

Once either rule is broken, the water is muddied as to the real intentions of the policeman or the suspect. If you make a policeman angry by being belligerent, or by not following his instructions, things can get out of control in a hurry. Once things get out of control, it becomes a guess as to whether the officer's actions were based on anger, race, problems at home, or something else. The only reasonable way to assert racism is to follow the two rules I described and then any real racism will become identifiable.

I want to present you with a real-life scenario that demonstrates the elements of hypersensitivity; refusal to follow a policeman's instructions; and being belligerent to a policeman. The incident I am referring to is the one between a black Harvard University professor and a white Cambridge, Massachusetts policeman.

The information I will present was acquired by reading the professor's bio, the police report of the incident, and by talking with a person that had spent some time with the professor. The professor has taught African- American Studies at Harvard University for a number of years. Teaching a course where you routinely discuss poor race relations, discuss legitimate cases of blacks being victimized, and cite numerous cases of racial dis- crimination have hypersensitized the professor on racial issues. The professor's hypersensitivity to race issues was demonstrated almost immediately after the police- man arrived at his house. When the policeman asked the professor to come outside, the professor answered, "Why, because I'm a black man in America?" This is the response of a hypersensitized individual who is displaying perceived racism. This is also an arrogant statement and a statement of disrespect. I searched for a reputable person that had spent time with this Harvard professor. I was fortunate in locating a college professor that was willing to give me his opinion. The only question I posed for my source was his perception of the professor's arrogance. He confirmed that the professor often presented himself as an arrogant person.

The professor is trained from his classroom teachings to see racism in situations where other people don't see it. There are a couple of other things I attribute to the professor flying off the handle with little provocation. He was already angry before the policeman showed up because he had locked himself out of his house. The professor stated that the policeman had come to his house because of racial profiling. The policeman was at the professor's house in response to a 9–1-1 call. The 9–1-1 caller indicated that there was a possible break-in at the professor's house but said nothing about race. When the policeman showed up at the residence, he queried the first person he met, namely, the professor. Because the professor was asked to come out of his house, he claimed the policeman was there based on racial profiling. That's what hypersensitivity will do to a person. The fact that the professor ended up in handcuffs was of his own doing. He remained belligerent the entire time, based on his false assumptions of racism. If he had not read racism into the policeman's initial actions, things could have been resolved rather quickly. Hypersensitivity can really mess things up.

The two guidelines I established—complying with a policeman's instructions and avoiding becoming belligerent with the policeman—are designed to help differentiate between real racism and perceived racism. They are also designed to help identify hypersensitivity that distorts reality. The Harvard professor broke both of my guidelines and thus skewed any further assessments of racism. I can understand the policeman's reluctance to issue an apology for his actions. He became a victim in this situation by being falsely accused of racism before all the facts were in.

I would like to retire the term *racial profiling* in favor of the simple term *profiling* or maybe *comprehensive profiling*. Most crimes are solved by combining multiple sources of evidence, thus the term comprehensive profiling seems appropriate.

There are rogue policemen whose actions really mess up race relations. While most policemen are honest enforcers of the law, there are some that are not. When the dishonest policemen get caught in racial acts, it tarnishes all policemen and blurs the line between real racism and perceived racism.

I asked a border patrol agent about profiling. He denied that the border patrol uses profiling. What this meant to me is that they have to dress things up a bit so that profiling is not obvious. I live fifty miles from the Mexican border. I routinely see border patrol vehicles parked in the interstate medians. I'm thinking to myself, if the border patrol does not use profiling, how do these guys know who to pull over? Are they expecting some vehicles to drive by with signs that say "Illegal Immigrants—Catch Us If You Can"? If not, then they have to be profiling. To avoid the appearance of profiling the border patrol pulls people over for having a tail light out or for making an improper lane change. This gives them an opportunity to look inside the vehicles. Once they look inside, they can root out any illegal immigrants. There are other vehicles that pass by that have a tail light out or make an illegal lane change that never get pulled over because they do not fit the profile for illegal immigrants. This means that the border patrol agents are profiling. But wait. The border patrol knows this, and so they occasionally ticket a vehicle that obviously contains no illegal immigrants just to prove that they do not profile. It's all just a ridiculous game of dis- guising what they're doing well enough to win in court.

Let's say that you are looking for some bad guys. You have two groups of one hundred people each. In one group, there are a lot of people that have the same traits as the last fifteen bad guys you apprehended. In the other group, there are very few people that look or act like the bad guys you apprehended. How are you going to proceed? I don't understand why profiling has such a negative con- notation when you are just trying to catch the bad guys. What's wrong with improving your chances by looking in places where you have had good luck before? That's what fishing is all about, isn't it—profiling the fish? It seems to me that minorities can do things that the majority would be in trouble for doing the same thing. I once saw an announcement in a newspaper for a meeting of a "Black Lawyers

Association." Apparently all the black lawyers in town had gotten together to form a civic group. I started thinking about what would happen if the announcement had been for a "White Lawyers Association." It would have created tremendous outrage. The same can be said of many other situations.

Discrimination has an extremely negative connotation. Is there such a thing as good discrimination? Of course there is. Let's say that four people apply for a job. The three not selected were victims of discrimination, right? Yes, but hopefully they were discriminated against for the right reasons. Those three people might have been discriminated against based on education, training, job experience, and other factors deemed appropriate for the selection process. Inappropriate discrimination would be based on factors such as sex, age, marital status, race, and those kinds of things. As an employer, particularly as an entrepreneur, is it okay for you to hire a person based on your perception of who will make you the most money? Is it possible that this selection factor (personal choice) should outdo all the other factors combined? Many capitalists would say yes. It is possible, however, that you will be accused of discrimination because other people with better resumes were not hired.

Any time I select one thing over another, I have discriminated against the thing not chosen. In choosing steak over chicken, I have discriminated against chicken. So how do we define what is legitimate discrimination and what is not? There was a creed my

ROTC cadets recited before every class. It said, "We will not lie, steal, or cheat, nor tolerate among us anyone who does." If only we could all live this way. When I cited the following example in my class, my students all said that lying was involved. My example was that of a lady walking into a room full of women and asking, "How do you like my new outfit, girls?" The women all raved about the out- fit even though many thought that it was dreadful. My students cited this as a case of lying. I redefined lying as being untruthful in such a way that you have something to gain for doing it. I thought about applying this same kind of reasoning to discrimination. It is your intent that determines whether or not you are discriminating, but it is the opinion of the other person that determines what the consequences will be.

I recall a situation that happened a few years back when I was an ROTC summer camp instructor. One of my male colleagues had given a really great lecture to the cadets. At the end of the lecture, a female cadet approached him and said she was going to turn him in to the camp commander for being sexist. Apparently, she had graded the lecture based on how often my colleague used he in a positive or negative light and how often he had used she in a positive or negative light. According to her score sheet, my friend used he more often in positive situations and used she more often in negative situations. After soliciting an apology from my colleague, she decided to not report him to the camp commander. I wish she had gone to the camp commander as I knew him pretty well. He would have told her that there is no place in the Air Force for people with the mindset she was displaying.

The large number of cultures in the United States is touted as being a strong asset to our country. I can see where it will eventually be a great asset when all the races and cultures have melded together. The various cultures have not yet melded enough to make combining cultures the asset that is touted. Right now, the multicultural effect in this country is creating many problems. I believe that much of what is seen as discrimination and racism are cultural differences. It seems reasonable to me that we can stop putting "origin of race" on application forms. There is already enough mixing of the races that "What race are you?" is a serious problem for many people to answer. Ebonics is an African-American vernacular that is an alternate form of English akin to jargon or slang. The Oakland, California school district wanted to recognize Ebonics an official language a few years ago but backed down when the backlash was overwhelming. Adopting Ebonics as an acceptable language in school just seems like an excuse for not learning proper English. Blacks are trying to gain more acceptance in the white community, but things like Ebonics are a step backward. I remember when I was in high school. My social circle developed its own lingo. We made up all kinds of words to substitute for the King's English. The difference between what we did and Ebonics is that we never lost sight of the English language. We retained our ability to use correct English when we needed to. I'm not sure the pro-Ebonics people can make this same statement.

Anecdotes

It's now halftime. If you need to go to the bathroom or get something to eat or drink, this is the time to do it. If you want to make this a true halftime, you need to change ends by sliding down the sofa or changing to another recliner.

1. If a suicide bomber survives his mission, what kind of punishment should the courts give him? Surely not the death penalty!
2. Football has one idea that I really like. When things are going really bad, you just drop back fifteen and punt. You don't even have to wait until fourth down. Life needs to have an equivalent.
3. America is the only place in the world where we will delay a criminal's execution because he is not well enough to go through with it. It's true!
4. Can a deaf schizophrenic "hear voices"?

5. Many cities now use photo-radar in order to catch speeders and issue tickets. The courts in Arizona have ruled that the pictures have to be clear enough to identify both the license plate and the driver to be enforceable. The run on Halloween masks has been unbelievable.
6. If you think you've got the world by the tail, look out. The world is a multi-tailed animal. While you've got a hold of one tail, the others are bopping you up "side of your head."
7. Sometimes it seems like bears are the only ones that have things figured out. They just sleep away the winter and wake up one hundred pounds lighter. Perfect!
8. Lying, stealing, and cheating are not a function of your character. They are a function of your habits.
9. I love describing typical Americans "getting away from it all." They take an RV out to commune with nature. While they are getting away from it all, they have a TV, a microwave, a shower, and air conditioning. What a great way to commune with nature and leave city life behind.
10. As I drive around the state of Arizona, I see signs for rivers; I drive across bridges; but I never see any water. I have concluded that Arizona is a place where they have to mow the rivers twice a year.

11. When I arrived in New Mexico, I was shocked to hear the natives refer to all soft drinks as cokes. I always thought coke meant Coca Cola. What really threw me for a loop was the first time my cadets operated a concession stand at a football game. People would order a coke. My cadets would respond with, "What kind of coke do you want?" The customer would then answer, "Orange." This is how it went all night, and it drove me nuts.
12. If you take something from someone without their knowledge, it is not stealing as long as you needed it more than the person you took it from. He was giving it to you; he just didn't know it. (A quote from one of my students who was totally serious).
13. Rome wasn't built in a day, but they didn't have power tools.
14. I spoke with an acquaintance about Arizona's water problems. He stated that the water problems were exaggerated as we were sitting on top of a hundred-year water table. My response to him: "How much water will we have in a hundred years?"
15. A customer in a restaurant asks the waitress if they have a diet meal. After the waitress indicates that they do, the man says, "I'll take two."
16. Polls show that men would rather marry a woman who is not "too experienced," yet these

same men are out there every weekend trying to create a shortage in this category.

17. What do people do when they can't sleep in the middle of the night? They watch TV. They are forced to watch infomercials on virtually every channel. These infomercials try to sell you absolutely everything—everything except sleep aids!
18. I have one basic rule for eating. I don't eat anything I can't pronounce.
19. People who visit the desert are often not impressed. It's only after they learn that deserts are created by too much good weather that their opinions change a bit.
20. I could never be president because I lack one quality that is absolutely essential. This quality is that you have to like cuisines from all over the world. I am too picky and would probably destroy our relationships with other countries by declining their food in favor of hamburgers and peanut butter sandwiches.
21. The Bible tells us that money is the root of all evil. Policemen and judges will tell you that the lack of money is the root of all evil.
22. I revel when I hear parents say to their children, "Act your age." What they really mean is, "Stop acting your age." Usually, the children are acting appropriately for their age but the parents can't stand it.

23. When I am giving full consideration to starting a diet, I remember the saying, "Fat and jolly; lean and mean." I then make the instant decision to be jolly.
24. I once asked a fellow how his life was going. He responded that his life was like being addicted to something he was allergic to.
25. I have always wondered why animals have tails while humans do not. I think I have come up with the answer. No T.P. in the wild.
26. Drug testing in professional sports has become common- place but common sense has to take control somewhere. I saw where competitors were drug tested at a chess tournament. My guess is that officials were testing for drugs that keep players awake. What else could it be?

Our Legal System the Good, the Bad, and the Ugly

No book critiquing the American society would be complete without a chapter on lawyers. Lawyers are outstanding at creating their own business. They remind me of bars and churches in that they can never go out of business. People will always find a reason to drink. They drink when they're uptight; they drink when they're loose. They drink when they get promoted; they drink when they get fired. They drink when they're mad; they drink when they're sad. People can always find a reason to drink. Bars can never go out of business if they are properly managed. As for churches, they are the ones that create sin and they are the ones that can take it away. If all businesses could operate like churches and bars, they would be quite prosperous.

Such is the nature of lawyers. As long as lawyers

can chase ambulances, they will never have to worry about employment. The contemporary ambulance chasers are lawyers that advertise class-action law suits on TV and want you to get on board for some easy money—money you deserve. Just call the number on your TV screen if you have any symptoms similar to the ones scrolling down or across your screen. If you have been injured in a car accident, you qualify for a lawsuit without even having to look at a list on your screen. Have you been fired from your job? You are also ripe for bringing a lawsuit against your former employer. If you go back thirty years, doctors and lawyers were not allowed to advertise on TV. I guess it would make them look bad if they had to drum up business. That's how the term "ambulance chaser" came to be. If lawyers could not advertise in order to create business, then they had to chase ambulances to the hospitals to get some business. This might be a bit of a stretch but certainly not a gross one.

Let's take a look at product liability lawsuits. Manufacturers created the lawsuits by putting products on the market that were dangerous or poorly made. Lawyers came to the rescue and forced manufacturers to be more responsible. If things had progressed to only this level, lawyers' reputations would be much better today.

I recall a lawsuit involving a woman who became very ill because she put KY jelly on her toast. When the word got out, an army of lawyers descended on this lady for the opportunity to represent her in court.

The results of the trial were that this lady was awarded a few hundred thousand dollars and the manufacturer was ordered to put a warning label on their packaging. It seems to me that anyone who would put KY jelly on their toast probably can't read the warning label anyway, so what's the point? This kind of lawsuit probably opened the eyes of a lot of lawyers to let them know that frivolous lawsuits are everywhere if you just look for them. Consumer ignorance coupled with a crafty lawyer is a winning combination.

I agree with juries when they level millions of dollars in penalties against large companies for marketing faulty or dangerous products. You have to hit these companies hard in the pocketbook when they act irresponsibly; however, just because a jury awards a ten million dollar judgment against a large corporation doesn't mean that the other side should be the beneficiary of ten million dollars. The amount of money received by the winning side should be unrelated to the amount forfeited by the losing side. The amount of money received by the winning side should be based on its own merits. It makes sense to give the claimant a reasonable share of the judgment, pay the lawyer his fair share, and give the rest to charity or pay down the national debt. If juries made reasonable awards in civil cases, I'm not sure that I would feel this way; but juries hand out huge awards like it was play money.

Another issue that is mediated through the courts is pain and suffering. Lawyers bring lawsuits based on their clients' pain and suffering. Is there anybody out there that hasn't endured pain and suffering? I'm sorry if you have not been fortunate enough to associate your pain and suffering with some company or individual so that you can win a lawsuit. Let's compare two cases of pain and suffering. In the first case, an individual has pain and suffering from an automobile accident where the other driver was at fault. Compare this situation with a case where a person's pain and suffering is from cancer. Both people are suffering physical and emotional pain. However, in the first situation (auto accident) the person can win a lot of money in a lawsuit. In the second situation (cancer patient), the victim does not receive any money for her pain and suffering but instead pays money for her pain and suffering. Maybe we can devise a system where we take some of the money from the first case and donate it to the cancer patient whose pain and suffering costs money instead of receiving money.

I sometimes wonder what can be done to renovate our justice system. Everybody complains about it, but you could never get enough accord to get anything done. If I could change just one thing about our legal system, it would be to allow common sense to permeate it. There are times when a jury finds a defendant guilty and then the case gets thrown out for some minor technicality. There has to be a way to put some common sense into situations like this. I saw a case where a guy was found guilty of a terrible crime and the verdict was thrown out because the grand jury that recommended him for trial had not been properly instructed. I can only guess as to the incorrect procedure but I do know that these kinds of situations can occur based on some incredibly minute mistake. It seems as though our legal system is a game between the prosecuting and defense attorneys. It is not a game. We are supposed to be getting to the truth about what happened in order to determine the guilt or innocence of a defendant. I really don't care whether the grand jury was instructed properly or not, unless it was a gross mistake. Our judicial system is broken if this kind of thing can happen. If there is no direct or indirect way it could change the outcome of the trial, the verdict should stick. I found another case involving a prison inmate who was being given a new trial because the jury had not been given their oath. It's not possible that a juror would vote differently had they recited the oath. Our judicial system is broken when it allows for this kind of reasoning.

The search and seizure laws are intended to keep somebody from searching your house without probable cause. It has grown from this to some ridiculous interpretations of the law that allow guilty people to go free. These technicalities that cause valid evidence to be thrown out go too far in protecting people who were caught red-handed. A response I would expect from some people is that I would feel differently if I was the accused person. If you live a clean life and have nothing to hide, you don't fear the long arm of the law. Most interpretations of the law work in favor of the guilty, not the innocent. What we should be accomplishing with our penal system is to put guilty people in jail and to keep innocent people out of jail. There is no criminal justice system we can devise that can accomplish precisely that. Sometimes people do despicable things but cannot be charged with a crime because they did not violate any existing law. Our lawmakers react to these kinds of situations and pass laws to nail the next guy for doing the same thing.

The legal expression of "innocent until proven guilty" has a very narrow application. This concept stems from the Constitution, but it only applies to a court of law. Outside of the legal system, you are usually considered guilty until proven innocent. Few people (except family and friends) will give you the benefit of the doubt until you are exonerated in a court of law. Basically, you are guilty until proven innocent. Let's say that you are an accountant. If your boss thinks that you have stolen money from the company, you will lose your job immediately. The boss is not going to let you continue to work while you are awaiting the results of a trial. It's too risky. You're considered guilty until proven innocent when you are outside the legal system.

A new situation has arisen among high school students called "sexting." This practice involves students sending pictures of themselves (minus some clothes) to other students via their cell phones. Sexting is akin to a teenage version of playing doctor but uses cell phones instead of being co-located. Some district attorneys have gone public about charging these students with sex crimes, charges that would label them as sex offenders for the rest of their lives. These district attorneys need to quit researching the legal statutes long enough to understand how their actions are going to affect these students. These district attorneys are not in favor of tempering the law with common sense. The only thing they seem to understand is how to prosecute people to make a name for themselves. They are proposing to ruin these students' lives based on some pretty innocent stuff. If these students are found guilty of committing sex crimes, they will have a felony on their records and will have to register as sex offenders. Being labeled a registered sex offender is a life-changing event that is worse than going to prison. Most people eventually get out of prison and put their lives back together, but being a registered sex offender is for a lifetime. Registered sex offenders have to check in with the police every time they relocate, even if the move is just down the street. Their neighbors will be informed that a sexual predator has moved into the neighborhood. The neighbors of sex offenders will tend to condemn them before they even meet them, based on their ignorance and prejudice.

I have an aunt who lives in a trailer park. A registered sex offender moved into her neighborhood a few months ago. The obligatory fliers were handed out to warn all the neighbors that a convicted sex offender had moved into the neighborhood. Without knowing anything about this person, some residents want him booted from the park—a typical response. These people condemned their new neighbor before they had even met him. This man was the victim of irrational fear. If the residents that wanted this man booted from the park would meet him and learn more about his situation, they might feel differently about him. Sex offenders need a strong support system, and having a good relationship with their neighbors is a key component of that support system.

I want to relate a story that explains why so many people are down on lawyers. I saw a lawyer on 60 Minutes who boasted that he had represented over one thousand clients arrested for drunk driving and that he had won every case. He made a lot of money for himself and exploited our porous legal system. This lawyer could care less if his clients were guilty or not. To him, it was just a game. He demonstrated how our judicial system is not set up to determine guilt or innocence. Guilt or innocence is not the objective. Lawyers defend clients they know are guilty and just consider it as part of the job. Most people could not do that. I understand that a defense lawyer's job is to do whatever it takes to get the jury to usher in a not-guilty verdict. I wonder what it feels like to win a case knowing that your client committed the crime and that he retains the capability of becoming a repeat offender.

You sometimes hear about defendants pleading insanity as a defense. Most of us cannot understand this defense unless the defendant had been documented as insane prior to committing the crime. The idea that someone is sane prior to committing a crime, becomes insane long enough to commit a crime, and then becomes sane again is not understandable. Let me interject some ways of viewing this situation. Most mental illnesses are not full-time illnesses. By this, I mean that most mentally ill people have good days and bad days, just like the rest of us. However, their bad days are much more dramatic, so they get labeled as mentally ill. Another point that needs to be recognized is that most people with mental illness are never diagnosed. They are often dismissed as just being "off the wall." Mentally ill people will usually deny their illness even when presented with solid evidence. What this means is that there are a lot of undiagnosed mentally ill people walking around. Let's say that one of these undiagnosed people commits a murder. The person has actually been mentally ill all along but did not have a diagnosis. What happens in court is the defense lawyer asks for a psychological evaluation. When the defendant is found to be mentally incompetent, there is a public outrage. If the crime is particularly heinous—let's say abduction and murder of a child—the outrage will be maximized. When the insanity plea is used, people will cry out that this is just a cop-out. People are outraged when a defendant has no prior diagnosis of mental illness until it pops up in court.

I have another way of looking at the mental illness issue. I submit that we are all schizophrenic, bipolar, have borderline personality disorder, or are in a state of depression to some degree. Nobody is the same person every day. We all get "off center" from time to time. It's just a matter of degree. It's those days where everything seems to go wrong; you don't feel like yourself. There are days when you break things, forget things, make poor decisions, or act inappropriately. Personally, I think that all people are out of their minds when they commit murder. Nobody can be in their right mind and murder someone. Do you remember the lady in Houston who drowned her five children? At the trial, it was deduced that she had to be sane at the time of the murders because she dialed 9–1-1 right after committing the murders. Let me describe two situations and you tell me which situation involves a sane person and which one involves an insane person. (1) A person commits murder and then dials 9–1-1. (2) A person commits murder and then goes on the lam. Which person is the sane person, and which one is the insane one? I can see a sane person doing either one, and I can see an insane person doing either one. This was a major point in this lady's trial. The prosecution made the point that the defendant had to be sane to call 9–1-1 after committing the murders. I don't see that. This lady had a history of mental illness prior to committing the murders. What reason does a mother have to kill her five children other than the fact that she was insane? ***Maybe we could do better on trials involving mental competency if we purposely put a couple of psychiatrists on the jury instead of just putting them on the witness stand.*** This seems like a giant improvement to our criminal justice system to me. I remember when postpartum depression and spousal abuse were not valid excuses for murdering family members. In looking back, we have to wonder how naïve and insensitive we were. Someday, we will view the court issues of today and wonder how naïve and insensitive we were back in the good old days of 2010.

Sociopolitical issues

I once watched a tape of a Philadelphia city bus crash. The tape showed people jumping off the bus, but it also showed people jumping on the bus. The people jumping on the bus had instantly recognized an opportunity to become part of a winning lawsuit, and so they went into their victim routine. Do you recall the case where a lady went through a McDonald's drive-through and spilled hot coffee in her lap? She sued McDonalds and won a substantial settlement. If spilling hot coffee in your lap is worth hundreds of thousands of dollars, where do you sign up? I want a piece of the action. These are not isolated events and people have taken notice of these get- rich-quick opportunities. Our society has gotten to the point that lots of people truly expect to come into a large sum of money at some point. Children's responses about what they want to be when they grow up have changed dramatically since I was a child. Children used to respond with answers like teacher, pilot, fireman, nurse, doctor, bus driver, farmer, etc. I witnessed a group of children on TV that were asked what they wanted to be when they grow up. I was astounded to hear each child provide the same answer—rich. They have been led to believe that they will come into some big money without having to work for it. They think they will win a lawsuit, receive a big inheritance, win the lottery, discover buried treasure, win big at the casino, etc. These children are in for a rude awakening. I think there are some adults that retain this same kind of thinking.

I grew up in Champaign, Illinois, home of the "Fighting Illini." The University of Illinois mascot was Chief Illinewek, probably the most revered sports symbol in all of college athletics. I got to watch the Chief perform about ten to twelve times a year while growing up. Even if the game score was dismal at halftime, Chief Illinewek would do his dance and whip the fans into a frenzy. Every school should be so lucky. Based on an NCAA ruling, Chief Illinewek has been forced into retirement; another case of a small minority overruling a large majority. A small number of Native Americans found the actions of Chief Illinewek to be degrading, and so they decided to take action. I feel certain that of all the people privileged enough to watch Chief Illinewek do his dance, no more than one percent would say that the Chief's dance was degrading. So why is Chief Illinewek out of business? The laws are written in ways that allow a very small minority to outdo the masses based mostly on emotion. I was watching CNN this morning as they announced the results of their latest poll. The poll queried the viewing audience about which societal issue they were most concerned. Sexual predators have been a newsworthy item over the past few weeks. Guess which issue was at the top of the poll? You got it: sexual predators. The poll results are always directly correlated to the amount of time spent on each subject. Change the amount of air time for various issues, and you change the results of the polls. If the news were to focus extensively on oil for three weeks, oil would replace sexual predators at the top of the poll. If the news focused extensively on ecology for three weeks, ecology would rise to the top of the polls. Conducting a poll using this method makes the information derived from the polls worthless. The only thing these polls prove is that the issue given the most air time will always be at the top of the polls. The correlation between air time and public opinion is a strong one. Lots of people do not have enough confidence to think for themselves. They want to be told how to think, and the media does exactly that.

TV is an incredibly dominant influence in most people's lives. The media possess the ability to change people's minds, so any strategies or mistakes the media make will reverberate across the country. TV presentations of the national news are often distorted or slanted in ways that mislead viewers. I saw a story on the news recently which reported that crime had dropped 20 percent in a particular area; however, the news coverage of crime in that area had increased by six hundred percent over the same period of time. Presenting this factual but unbalanced news to viewers makes it difficult for them to feel like the crime rate is going down. Another example of media distortion that comes to mind is the abduction of children. Child abductions have been played up by the media in such a way that parents are now afraid to let their children play in their front yard. Child abductions are not way up as the news leads you to believe but are actually down. What we see on the evening news needs to be tempered with our personal experiences and those of our family, friends, and neighbors. This gives us a better perspective than simply digesting the evening news at face value. An accurate assessment of your world is what you see out of your kitchen window. This perspective is more accurate than assessing your world through the national news on TV.

Competition between the various news media is very tight and I think it drives them to sensationalize news stories to attain better ratings. Near-truths or exaggerations sell better than honest reporting. Show me a journalist that doesn't jazz up her stories a little and I will show you a journalist that will either make some changes or will be looking for work in a different field. Journalism fits into the same mold as all the other college majors. There is a huge leap from college to the real world. When I graduated with a degree in accounting and got my first accounting job, I was awe-struck at how completely different my job was from the college courses I had taken. In talks I have had with engineers, pharma- cists, teachers, and other professionals, they all agreed that what they learned in college was fundamentally different from what they did on their jobs. What I think they were telling me is that college is "pure academics" while the real world operates in totally different ways, including being unethical. Academics are theory while the real world is the practice of theory.

Let's compare journalism academics with real-world journalism. When someone takes college journalism classes, he learns about "yellow journalism," the Freedom of Information Act, the need to protect his sources, and how to dig up information. I'm not sure how much journalism classes teach the kind of journalism that will satisfy one's future bosses. Their future bosses are going to want them to bend the rules in order to create company profit. If you scare the public, you get higher ratings. Therefore, as a journalist, you can either learn how to sensationalize and exaggerate reality or your competitors will pass you by. It's a shame that journalists have to alarm the public in an on-going basis in order to be the best that they can be.

The political nature of war changed with Vietnam, much of it based on journalism. Wars have traditionally been fought to acquire or occupy land. Vietnam was not fought over land. The enemy would gain land in a battle and then abandon it the next day. This strategy made our struggle more confusing and counter-productive. WWII went through a media-driven shock that changed people's attitudes about the war, only it wasn't in real time like Vietnam. When pictures of dead American soldiers started being published in newspapers and magazines after the start of WWII, it shocked the American public and galvanized them against our enemies. When graphic war scenes are broadcast on TV, it is much more compelling than still photographs shown weeks after the fact.

When the media broadcast the Vietnam War into people's homes, the effect of the broadcasts was the opposite of what it had been in WWII. Looking at dead American soldiers made Americans want to break off the fight and come home. The media, backed with its First Amendment rights, stoked the anti-war movement in a way that no other segment of our society could do. The North Vietnamese used this fact to their advantage. They devised a strategy to wait us out, knowing that our media were going to help them win the war. Broadcasting the war directly into people's living rooms created the impetus for anti-war protests which eventually led to our downfall on the battlefield. The media is exceedingly powerful; I would say too powerful. The only way of stopping the media is for the media to stop itself.

Broadcasting national and international news into our homes is very destructive to our mental health: the snipers in Maryland; the Oklahoma City bombing; child abductions; violence in the Middle East. Is it important for people to stay informed on world and national news? I advocate staying informed for several reasons but I can't say that happiness is one of them. The people that are the most knowledgeable about current events seem to be some of the biggest complainers. Staying informed might help these people's pocketbooks but it doesn't seem to make them any happier than less informed people. I think the term "ignorance is bliss" may have more truth than many informed people want to believe. When CNN broadcasts a national story, it comes across much more powerfully and dynamically than when your local news team broadcasts the same story. Because your local news teams broadcast mostly news about your home town, you develop a rapport with them that you don't develop with national broadcasters. When your local news station covers a tragic national event, the blow is softened because the news is delivered by people you know.

What would happen if we had a TV channel similar to CNN's Headline News, but with one major exception. The exception would be that this station aired only good news—no bad news allowed. The station could be called *All Good News All the Time*. Based on my under- standing of human nature, this channel would soon be off the air. People want to see the bad stuff. It's like put- ting a nice family movie on one TV channel and a bone- chilling, blood-curdling movie on another. Which one do you think will achieve the higher ratings? Human nature at its best!

I remember when teen pregnancy was strictly a family problem. Families absorbed the cost of teen pregnancies. Now we have social programs to deal with these situations. Problems that were traditionally family or community problems have become societal problems. How does this piece of the puzzle fit into a "smaller government?" People say that they want less government but every time they are in need, they ask, "Where's the government?" You can't have it both ways. People want the government when they need it and then want it to go away when they don't need it.

I once asked my ninety-year-old grandmother what she thought about taxes having risen so much over the years. Grandma has traveled the world several times over and even lived in India and Afghanistan for ten years. She was always very astute when it came to politics and still had a terrific memory at age ninety. In response to my query about rising taxes, she responded with this answer. She said that taxes were much lower years ago; however, she was quick to point out that you didn't get much for your taxes in those days and that the results of her tax dollars were not very perceptible. She went on to explain how much we get for our tax dollars today. We get a well-equipped military, a space program, interstate highways, national parks, Social Security, Medicare, and more. She spoke at length, comparing what we get for our tax dollars today versus what she got for her tax dollars back in the 1920s. Her point was that you get what you pay for. If people want to pay lower taxes, they have to expect to receive less government services. What do you say to getting rid of all the abuse and waste in the government and then lowering taxes accordingly? This would be an ideal way to conduct matters. Waste and abuse, to a large extent, are a function of the size of the organization. With the federal government being the largest entity in the world, it makes sense that it would have the most waste and abuse. The government does not have a lock on waste and abuse. Waste and abuse run rampant in large corporations as well. Corporate waste and abuse might well run proportionate to the federal government. If you knew how corporations spent their money, you would be shocked.

There is another way to look at waste and abuse, be it the government, a corporation, or even you. Oh yes, you too have waste and abuse. Think about it. Waste and abuse create jobs. They are a means of stimulating the economy. If everybody was waste-free, the economy would be in trouble. Being free of waste and abuse eliminates jobs. Show me a company that is extremely frugal with their money, and I'll show you a company where the employees are not happy. The company's frugality would likely permeate everything, including salaries, benefits, and perks. The company would probably have security cameras installed everywhere to ensure that nobody was stealing pencils or paper clips.

I want to shift your attention away from corporations and government and get back into our neighborhoods. Things are not always as they seem. We are all too judgmental, particularly in situations where we don't have enough information to make an expressed judgment. I have an example that illustrates how people make judgments without having enough facts. Suppose you are driving down the road and see your pastor coming out of a strip joint. I daresay that most parishioners would waste no time in smearing the pastor's reputation. You can't make that kind of judgment because you don't have enough information to draw an accurate conclusion. Suppose you find out later that the pastor had gone into the strip joint to try to save a parishioner or one of the bar employees. Wouldn't you feel awful if you had already smeared your pastor's name? As a rule of thumb, we all need to be less judgmental and slower to invoke it. People deserve to be given the benefit of the doubt until all the facts are in.

Along with being judgmental, we are all too impatient. This next example might describe you or some- body you have witnessed. A person is stuck in a long line of cars on a winding, two-lane highway. It is not prudent to pass. Invariably, you will see someone risk their life to move up one car in line. This driver risked everything to move ahead thirty feet. There are other situations that make no more sense than this one. What do you do when you are behind a car that is going 10 mph below the speed limit? Do you end up having a one-way conversation with the driver in front of you? It's something most of us have done. The reality is that over a six-mile distance, the difference between driving at the speed limit and driving 10 mph below the speed limit amounts to about one minute. What the heck were you going to do with that extra minute anyway?

Recent statistics that I was able to find in multiple sources on the Internet have led me to apply some common sense to arrive at a conclusion. The most successful people in our society are having significantly less children per capita than are less successful people. Success was measured only in terms of income. Successful people are having 1.8 children per couple while the less successful (disadvantaged?) people are having 4.2 children per couple. If this trend continues, there is an ominous problem on the horizon. History tells us that people born into poverty tend to remain in poverty. If we project the current statistics out for a few generations, the socio- economic situation becomes more problematic with each passing generation. The math just works that way. When each generation builds onto this model, the percentage of successful people becomes smaller with each generation while the percentage of people living in poverty expands with each generation. This is a recipe for disaster unless we can overcome it.

Do modern inventions serve to make us happy? Let's take the example of a person who buys a new Porsche. He parks his car at the far end of the parking lot to avoid getting dings from surrounding parked cars. He puts a cover over his car to avoid the damaging rays of the sun. He wants his boss to be understanding when he bolts from work at the slightest threat of a storm. The guy who owns a Porsche and then acts this way is pulling way too many weeds and not smelling enough roses. I think people who drive reliable, moderate-looking cars are happier than Porsche owners. They have greater peace of mind by not having to worry about where everybody else is parking or what the weather is doing.

I took a CPR class with about fifteen people a couple of years ago. The instructor stressed that we use a baggie-like barrier for protection while blowing air into a victim. After practicing mouth-to-mouth resuscitation for a while, the instructor gave us a scenario to think about. She asked us what we would do if we came across a person in dire need of CPR but we did not have a barrier to breathe through. Not one person in the class said that they would perform mouth-to-mouth resuscitation without a barrier except me. I couldn't believe that my classmates were all going to let this person die because there was a one-in-ten million chance they might con- tract AIDS or some other life-threatening illness. I don't understand that kind of thinking, but it seems that people have learned that running scared and over-reacting are acceptable responses. Running scared is the preparation stage for some unknown disaster, and over-reacting is the post-disaster stage. I feel certain that potential law- suits are the driving force behind this kind of thinking. Potential lawsuits cause people to make their decisions based on worst-case scenarios. Overreacting is a normal response by many people. If a person reacts normally or under-reacts, it is often interpreted by other people as a demonstration of not caring. You are supposed to over- react to demonstrate that you truly care.

Let's examine a couple of situations to see how men and women compare in identical situations. Suppose that a lady walks into a room of women and asks the group, "How do you like my new outfit?" All the women will rave about the outfit. Later, in private, many of these same women will express opinions that the outfit was dreadful. Now let's take the same situation for a man. Suppose that a guy walks into a room of men and says, "How do you like my new duds?" The responses could be anything from complimentary to snickers and howls. The value of this scenario is to demonstrate the different ways men and women express bonding. What about bonding on the golf course? With a foursome of men, there will be lots of put-downs, practical jokes, and telling it like it is (horrible). I have never observed this sort of thing happening among women golfers. When a woman hits a bad shot, the other women in her group will tell her that it was a nice shot. Women need to protect each other from emotional hurt while men welcome the verbal abuse as camaraderie.

This next issue really hits at the fiber of our country. If you go back a couple of generations, our priorities were much different. People's priorities were to fall in love and then look for a job wherever their sweetheart happened to be. Today, we put the premium on jobs over relationships. People's first priority is to find a good job; and once that is secured, they try to find that special someone who is co-located with their job. I guess the modern thinking is that it is harder to find a great job than it is to find a great spouse. Couple this aspect with the fact that both people in the relationship have careers and managing relationships becomes difficult. When one marriage partner receives a job transfer, the non-transferred spouse is forced to make a choice between their career and their marriage. All too often the career is selected. It would be nice if we once again started prioritizing people above jobs. This country would be a happier place to live.

How do you answer people who ask, "Why do you drive that car?" or "Why do you go to church?" or "Why do you eat the food you do?" Usually, you try to come up with some sort of logical or scientific answer that will, no doubt, be challenged by the other person. Well, I have the perfect answer for you that will work in nearly every situation. In response to any challenge, simply say, "Because it makes me happy." What kind of come-back can the other person have to that response? This response does not work in every situation. When you ask your son why he has such low grades, you definitely don't want to hear a response of, "Because it makes me happy."

Family dynamics play a large role in your belief system. I have never heard of a family described as functional. I guess all families are dysfunctional to one degree or another. I taught high school in a very dysfunctional town. I used to joke with people that many of my students had their family reunions at the state prison so that they could maximize attendance. I tested my students by laying out an unusual situation for them. I explained to my students that if I knew my brother had committed murder and it was in no way justifiable, I would turn him in to the police. My students gasped. “You don’t turn in family,” they said in unison. My response to them was in two parts: (1) Just because it was my brother who com- mitted the crime doesn’t make him above the law any more than anybody else, (2) I told my students that my brother knows that I would turn him in for murder and I know that he would turn me in for murder. Because we both know this, neither of us is going to commit murder and expect our family to protect us. I’m not sure the students understood what I was getting at, but I hope that I was able to plant a few seeds. I told my students that it is important to hang out with the right kind of people. “If you hang out with bums, you’ll be a bum. If you hang out with scholars, you’ll be a scholar.” Many teenagers are arrested just because they were along for the ride when the driver of the car committed a crime. The boys and girls that were just along for the ride end up with criminal records just for hanging out with the wrong people.

I saw a very sad case on TV that involved some good kids that went joy riding with a driver of poor character. The driver impulsively decided to rob a convenience store and ended up murdering the clerk. The kids in the car didn’t even know that the driver was going to rob the store, much less kill the clerk. The good kids in the car were tried as accessories to murder and were sentenced to prison. When teenagers hang out with the wrong people, they might only be guilty of poor judgment, but their criminal record will reflect something different.

Commitments of all types are waning in this country. Companies and employees are not as loyal to each other as they once were. People live together instead of getting married. I want to use my high school students to explain how they view commitment. They get a phone call on Tuesday evening about a babysitting job on Friday. They don't confirm or deny that they will take the job but just say that it sounds good and they will get back later. After asking around a little bit, I found out that this is nor- mal procedure for teenagers today. You don't commit to something the first time it is offered. You tentatively say yes and then shop around to see if you can do better. My students enlightened me that Tuesday was much too early to make a commitment for Friday. I asked them, "Can you put yourself in the other person's shoes?" The other people need to know whether or not they are going to have a babysitter for Friday night. The response I got from my students was that they would keep trying to find another sitter. They didn't see their noncommittal actions as being inconsiderate. It's just the way the game is played. I probed to determine at what point they could commit for a Friday evening babysitting job. They told me that the latter half of Thursday evening would be a point where they could feel comfortable making a commitment. I just wonder if these students approach dating the same way for a weekend date. I guess you are sup- posed to tentatively commit for a Friday date on Tuesday and then try to come up with something better.

If you come up with something better, you go with the better offer and call the first person back to cancel.

For a person who is a strong believer in commitment, I find this method of quasi-commitment a bit difficult to swallow. I am not naïve enough to think that teenagers can make commitments like adults, but I don't remember my teenage friends or me having a problem with relatively simple commitments.

I had a good friend in the Air Force who retired about five years before I did. He bought a hardware store in another state. I decided to drop in on him a couple of years later to see how he was doing. I really wanted to know what it was like being out in the civilian world. I asked my friend what was the biggest difference between the Air Force and the civilian world. I couldn't believe how quickly he responded. He related some things to me that were about commitment. He said that he didn't realize the level of commitment Air Force people had. When people in the Air Force were given an assignment, you could count on it being done correctly, on time, and with pride. My friend said that he wished the people that worked in his store were the same way. He said that his employees tried to do as little as possible; they were habitually late or sometimes didn't show up at all; they stole things from the store; and they quit with regularity. I asked my friend why he didn't just fire the employees that were not good workers. He said that he did that a lot when his store first opened but he often ended up working the store by himself. He decided that it was better to have lousy workers than to not have any.

I sense that many people are confused about contemporary issues. When one person makes a definitive statement based on research and then another person conducts a study that contradicts the first study, it 's like "crying wolf " to the public. Are you confused about food, diet plans, and diet supplements? You should be. It 's impossible to determine which avenue to take when you are trying to eat healthier and lose weight. Are you confused about how to invest your money? There are hundreds of people trying to persuade you that they have the answer. After experiencing enough situations like this, people are not going to heed anything they hear or read.

I once saw two quasi-related articles side-by-side in the newspaper. One article stated that Americans are living longer than ever. The other article stated that Americans are fatter than ever. I can see how someone puts two and two together and arrives at the conclusion that being fat will lengthen their life! To add to the confusion, I recall reading an article in the newspaper that suggested that being a little overweight is good for you.

Professional sports are the epitome of non-commitment. It is common these days for team owners to give ultimatums to public officials in the cities where they play. "Give me a new stadium, or I'll move my team to another city." This sort of blackmail has created many controversies, disenchanted fans, and created financial hardships on sponsoring cities. I remember stadiums that were built in the 1960s and 1970s that were beautiful places to watch football and baseball games. Now these stadiums are being demolished to give into owners' demands for new stadiums. Players do the same sort of thing. "Double my salary, or I'll go somewhere else." Money rules over loyalty in most situations. This is a sad commentary on our society.

Another aspect of professional sports in which commitment is an issue is the owners versus the players. The players have gone on strike several times over the years as a means of increasing their pay. The players say they should be paid a lot of money because they are responsible for putting fans into the seats. I personally see players as high-priced employees. Being a professional athlete is a job. If players lose their jobs, they will have to go to work for a living just like the rest of us. The owners have huge amounts of money invested in their teams. When things go bad, who loses? It's the owners. The players' salaries are guaranteed. It's only fair that the ones that stand to lose the most if things go bad should be the ones who profit the most when things go good.

If players have a bad season, have you ever heard of them demanding to renegotiate their contracts for less pay? Never! However, if players have great seasons, they want to renegotiate their contracts upward. The players have got it made. I recall one incident where a player did the honorable thing. It was Lymon Bostock of the then California Angels. When he performed terribly the first month of the season, he felt guilty about being paid so much and not living up to it. He decided to return his salary for that month to the team, but the team wouldn't take it. So he donated his month's salary to charity. I wish that sort of thing would happen more often. It shows real character. The players are greedy and have no problem jumping from team to team for more money. Loyalty is nonexistent. The same could be said of owners, but I see a distinction between making a business decision (owners trading a ballplayer) and just going for the money (players).

I calculate that some pro baseball pitchers are making $15,000 per pitch! If players want a bigger share of the pie when things are going good, they should be willing to suffer more when things go bad. Most players (employees) are not willing to live under those rules. This is why players have a guaranteed salary and the company (team owner) has all the risk. Owners, I'm on your side.

When I was growing up, I always thought there were some things that would never change. You know what I'm talking about—things like weddings, churches, and funerals. Well, there is one ritual that seems about as sacred as it gets, and yet it is making some changes that blow me away. What I am referring to is funerals. The routine usually includes things like obituaries, funeral home visitations, memorial services, eulogies, and burial or cremation. I have seen some bizarre variations of these rituals, such as having your ashes sucked through a jet engine or having a wild party for the deceased. Those behaviors don't really bother me too much because I see them more as individual variations, or creative juices run wild. I don't see them as societal swings. There is one variation of funeral rituals that you have to see to believe. There are now funeral homes that offer drive-through viewings of the deceased. In my opinion, drive-throughs are for banks and fast food, not funeral homes. If you are too busy to park your vehicle and go inside the funeral home to pay your respects, then just forget it. People who go through funeral home drive-throughs are not paying their respects to the deceased; they are just satisfying their morbid curiosity.

When I was a kid, the obituaries were much shorter than they are today; and there were no pictures. The obituaries were considered as public service announcements, and newspapers did not charge for the service. Now newspaper companies see obituaries as commerce and not as a service; hence, a hefty charge is made for obituaries. The pictures in the obituaries are interesting. Some obituary pictures are much younger-looking than the deceased looked at the time of their death. It makes me wonder if the person arranging the obituary did not have a current picture; or if they wanted the person to be remembered as the younger person they once were; or if the deceased had been in poor health for some time and their last photos would not do them justice. I did see one picture in the obituaries that left little doubt as to what his family's thinking was. The picture they selected for his obituary was his mug shot!

People want to be loved unconditionally. That's what makes us feel good about life. This is where pets enter the picture. Pets will love you unconditionally. They don't care if you're an alcoholic, can't hold a job, or if your house is always a mess. It's hard for people to do that. People rightly expect certain behaviors from each other. Relationships crumble when these expectations are not met. It is easy to see how dogs got to be "man's best friend." Dogs will love you unconditionally, even when people will not.

There is a sociological trend that has been emerging for a number of years that can't possibly last. People are living longer but are retiring earlier. After a while, the math just doesn't add up. People will retire when they are forty-five and live to be one hundred and twenty. Seventy-five years in retirement? That can't be. Would people really want to live to be one hundred and twenty if they were required to work until they were one hundred? The math works out better that way, but I don't think people will buy it.

A social issue that is troublesome to me is political advertisements. There is nothing to prevent a candidate from distorting the truth about his opponent. Candidates can say anything they want and make it stick. By the time a person sees three months of negative advertising about two competing candidates, they don't want to vote for either one. So what is the solution to this problem? I suggest that we appoint an independent council of six people who are selected based on their longtime display of integrity, candor, and trustworthiness. These people are the kind who could get eighty percent of the vote if they were running. We could use this council to screen all political ads before they were aired to insure they are not distorted or misleading. If an ad doesn't pass inspection, it never gets aired. This kind of system might do wonders for turned-off voters. Political ads are currently not a viable way of ascertaining who the best candidate is.

As you have probably detected, I am down on political correctness in lots of situations. Several years ago, a law was enacted to force public facilities to put diaper changing tables in men's and women's restrooms. The only reason we force businesses to install changing tables in men's restrooms is to be politically correct. Did there used to be men who were outraged because there weren't changing tables in the restrooms? In all the times I have been in public restrooms, I have yet to see a single father using the diaper changing table. Many men would be happy to change the diaper in the car. This way they can use the lack of a diaper changing table as an excuse to leave the store. The amount of money we waste to ensure political correctness is absurd.

I have another political correctness situation that seems to border on the absurd. Towards the end of my Air Force career, I started looking for one final job in the Air Force that would enhance my resume and hone my skills for civilian employment. After looking around for a while, I decided that being an ROTC instructor would be a good job to posture myself for civilian life. I began a search to find an ROTC job and found several advertised positions. I was on tap to drive 1600 miles to a family reunion the next week when I noticed that a couple of the advertised job openings were along my route. I decided to explore a couple of these universities to see what kind of reaction I might have. One of the universities I visited was an all-black school. While I was roaming around campus, I came across a bulletin board. There was a particular notice that caught my eye. The university was offering minority scholarships for white students. I had never thought of white students as minorities, but I guess they can be in some politically correct situations.

It's time to take a stand on illegal immigration. My plan is a simple one. The only solution I see to stopping illegal immigrants from entering this country is to build a wall that cannot be scaled over or tunneled under and have it run from San Diego to Brownsville, TX. I am now in trouble with the ecologists because this wall will interrupt the migration habits of some animals. My response to this is that animals are very resilient and have great survival instincts. The displaced animals will learn new survival skills and will adapt accordingly.

If we can build walls to keep prisoners in, surely we can build walls to keep illegal immigrants out. A wall solves half the problem. The other half is to tell the illegal immigrants that are already in the U.S., "Congratulations, this is your lucky day. You are now legal citizens of the United States." This would be a one-time good deal and would not be repeated for future illegal immigrants. We could then adopt a reasonable immigration policy that has fairness and continuity built in. We could begin accepting new immigrants in reasonable numbers. The immigrants would have to clear three hurdles to become U.S. citizens; (1) pass a background check in Mexico and the U.S., (2) be able to pass a test on U.S. politics and history; and (3) demonstrate proficiency in English.

Believe it or not, the illegal immigration issue might resolve itself in a couple of decades with no intervention at all. The way the U.S. economy is going, in twenty years, the Mexican economy may be doing better than the U.S. economy. At that point we will become the illegal immigrants trying to sneak into Mexico!!

Great coaches in any sport can always be counted on to impart wisdom to their players that transcend athletics. I want to provide you with some coaching tactics that I learned from John Wooden, arguably the greatest college basketball coach of all time. Coach Wooden had a way of making complex tasks seem simple. "We must be quick, but not in a hurry," was one of coach Wooden's sayings. Can it get any simpler than that? UCLA had some truly outstanding teams in the 1960s and 1970s. Those championship teams influenced many high school All-Americans to come to UCLA. Usually, these players brought their inflated egos with them; but Wooden knew exactly how to shrink these freshmen's heads back to size. I can only imagine the look on these freshmen's faces when coach Wooden spent their first practice teaching them how to wear their shoes and socks. It had occurred to Wooden during his many years of coaching that players were getting blisters because they didn't know how to put on their shoes and socks properly. The socks need to be stretched out tight so that they would not bunch up inside the shoe and create problems. The shoes need to be the correct size and laced up tight. It sounds simple, but I think it is a great starting point for incoming freshmen with big egos. It sets the tone for things to come.

UCLA had a rule in those days that everybody had to be clean shaven. If a coach tries to enforce this rule on his college players now, the ACLU will be sending the player their business card. On one occasion Bill Walton walked in with about ten day's growth on his face. Coach Wooden confronted Bill in a very nice way and reminded him about his rule on facial hair. Bill was the rebellious type and indicated that he wanted to keep his beard. Coach Wooden acknowledged that he understood Bill's stance and said that the team was really going to miss him. No argument. No hassle. The next day, Bill showed up clean shaven and all was forgotten. Time after time, Coach Wooden gave solid guidance in ways that created respect and devotion from his players.

I want to tell you a little bit about my grandfather. He was one of the pioneers of modern agriculture. He ushered in the age of fertilizer and crop rotation and demonstrated advanced farming techniques to American farmers. He then spent ten years in India and Afghanistan teaching farmers in those countries how to grow crops. I was really proud of him. Then one day my bubble got burst a little. Someone pointed out to me that my grandfather had created hardships for American farmers. I didn't understand what he was saying. This person explained to me that the U.S. traditionally exported a tremendous amount of grain to poor countries; but ever since my grandfather taught these other countries how to grow crops, they don't need to import grain from the U.S. like they used to. This creates hardships on American farmers.

My grandfather's biggest retirement hobby was growing prize roses. I think he had 108 rose bushes. After he had endured two heart attacks, he could tell that he wasn't going to last that much longer. He decided that his way of seeing everyone for what would probably be his last hurrah was to have a rose party. He invited family and friends from all over the country to attend. Grandpa's youngest brother lived about two thousand miles away and declined his invitation. Grandpa called his brother and asked why he wasn't coming. His brother said that he couldn't afford to come twice in a short period of time (rose party and funeral). Grandpa told his brother that if he could only afford to come once that he should come for the rose party. Grandpa said that it made more sense to come while he was alive than after he was deceased. With his point having been made, grandpa sent his brother the air fare to come to the rose party.

Implementing a federal sales tax in lieu of our current income tax system has been offered to the public but has never caught hold. A federal sales tax is the only method of taxation that generates tax revenue from money now hid- den from the IRS. Things like illegal drugs, prostitution, the black market, and other sources of money that are now hidden from the IRS would be taxed under a federal sales tax law when the money is spent at the stores.

Here are some of the aspects of the federal sales tax plan that I want you to understand:

1. The IRS could be shut down completely thus retiring a huge bureaucracy and saving $11.4 billion per year that it takes to operate it. (FY2009 est figure)
2. When there is no longer an income tax, there will be no need to file tax returns.
3. There would be no more cheaters on income taxes. This should increase government revenue and keep people out of a quandary as to whether the IRS will seek them out for an audit. There should be a corresponding decrease in the feeling that "big brother" is watching.
4. People should pay less federal tax after switching to a federal sales tax system. Since all money, legal or illegal, would be taxed at the stores, revenue generated from illegal drug sales, prostitution, black market sales, stolen money, etc. should equate to lower tax burdens for everyone.

To make the switch from an income tax system to a

sales tax system, there are some adjustments that need to be included with the change. Changing our current system where tax rates increase with increases in income to a system where everyone pays the same sales tax rate would cause the tax burden to shift toward lower-income people. There are several things that could be done to counter this injustice. I have two recommendations that would make the sales tax system fairer: (1) make food, drugs, and other daily necessities tax free; (2) exempt people on Social Security from all sales tax. There are other ways to tweak the system to ensure that poor people are not burdened beyond what is their fair share.

I recommend that the sales tax rate be examined yearly by the OMB (Office of Management and Budget) and that it submit any recommended sales tax rate change to Congress for approval.

If adopted, this new tax system should be implemented five years after it becomes law. This five-year waiting period will allow tax payers time to posture for the upcoming change and minimize any losses that occur as a result of the change.

The Workplace

I enjoyed writing this chapter the most. The workplace is always a great place to do some people-watching and draw conclusions.

I have taught a few college classes about workplace psychology and sociology. My students all worked during the day and went to college at night. They continually enlightened me with interesting tidbits about their workplaces. One of my students presented me with a piece of paper with a matrix on it. The title at the top of the page said, "Bullshit Bingo." He explained to me that his office staff meetings had become so boring that he had created a way to spice them up. On an ordinary bingo card, he had replaced the numbers with common workplace terms such as "think outside the box," or "be proactive," or "multitasking," or "do more with less," or "raising the bar." At staff meetings, he and some of his coworkers played "Bullshit Bingo." As these terms were spoken during the staff meeting, these company loyalists crossed them out on their bingo card. I don't know how they resisted yelling bingo during the meetings; but apparently, they had great restraint. What a great way to spice up corporate America!

I had many discussions with my students about dress in the workplace. It seems that work attire has been getting more and more relaxed during the past thirty years—that is, until recently. I suppose the fad had to reach a limit at some point and, apparently, dress policies are starting to swing back the other way. When I polled my students about dress policies, they responded with a variety of answers. They ranged from questioning management's sanity to saying that their employers didn't pay them enough to require them to dress nicely. Their rationale was interesting to say the least. Some students said that people do their best work when they feel comfortable. These students advocated a very casual dress code. Other students said that when you look good, you feel good, and thus become more productive. I put the following analogy to my students: If you were going to have open heart surgery, which doctor would you pick; a doctor who dresses professionally, or one who wears overalls and smokes a corncob pipe? The politically correct answer is that it shouldn't make any difference. However, most of the students preferred to trust their lives to the doctor that dresses professionally. Yet it could be that the nicely dressed doctor was working through some malpractice suits while the doctor that wore the overalls was one of the leading heart surgeons in the country. Next, I brought up the subject of people working in the public eye versus those who work in the back office. What is the point of dressing nicely if your co-workers are the only ones who see you? Some of the students who advocated dressing nicely all the time stuck to their guns; however, some of the "dress nicely all the time" students began to ease their standards. There seemed to be some consensus that employees who don't work in the public eye should be able to dress more casually than those who do.

Another topic of discussion was workplace décor. The thing that precipitated this discussion was a story I saw on the evening news. It seems that there was a company in California where the employees were able to decorate their work cubicles any way they wanted. One guy had a golf décor. He put down a putting carpet. He had clubs and balls all over the place. Golfing attire was prevalent. Another fellow had a military motif. He had camouflage netting everywhere. There were pictures of tanks and airplanes all over the walls. Upper management cited improved morale and productivity after making the switch to this policy.

I asked my students how many of them had recognition and incentive programs at their workplace. Most of them said they did. These kinds of things are very politically correct, and bosses receive lots of accolades for pushing them. According to my students, most of these programs are "eyewash" and have no affect on morale or productivity. I am referring to incentive programs such as Employee-of-the-Month, being awarded a temporary parking spot by the front door, and things of this nature. My students said that Employee-of-the-Month is an absolute joke and companies should be fined for doing it. The whole idea is meant to distribute the award so that eventually everybody wins (which everybody knows). Get rid of it.

Another issue in the workplace that needs some attention is promotions. It seems that the selection of whom to promote is more of a political decision than a managerial one. The promotion system for the Air Force has changed many times over the years. It is very difficult to compare a maintenance officer in Korea with a pilot from South Carolina for promotion. By law, only a certain number of officers can be promoted at each promotion board. Since the board has never met the officers, they rely on officers' records to tell them who to promote. What they look for are subtle messages found within the records, kind of like codes. One indicator that someone is really sharp is that they change jobs and locations frequently. Those officers are called "fast burners." They are so good that everybody wants these officers to work for them. This is easily perceptible by a promotion board. Changing jobs frequently is a tip to the promotion board that an officer is top notch.

Officers that are terrible at their jobs often look the same as the top-notch officers on paper. Nobody can stand to work with them and so they get moved around a lot. On paper it is difficult to tell the "fast burner" from the louse. You would think that their work evaluations would make it easy to distinguish one officer from the other; but oftentimes, they did not. You see, no one ever wants to be known as the guy who ruined somebody's career by giving him a bad evaluation. Each evaluator would write a superlative report on the louse and leave it up to the next evaluator to play the part of the "heavy," and the cycle kept repeating itself. Under a system like this, I saw many people get promoted who did not deserve it and I also saw a lot of people who deserved to be promoted get passed over. I don't know how promotions stack up in the civilian world, but from what I gather from my friends, there are a lot of injustices there as well.

Foreign Relations

I want for you to read the following article and draw your conclusions. To check the status of your open-minded- ness, I am keeping the name of the author secret until after you have formulated your opinions. I will reveal the identity of the author on the next page to see if it changes your thinking.

From the Associated Press:

> The U.S. has ushered in an era of imperialism responsible for many of the world's problems. Americans want so much to be the winners. The fact that we are sick with this illness, the winner's complex, is the main reason why everything in the world is so confused and complicated. The U.S. is in an aggressive, empire-building mood.

> This has led the U.S. to commit a string of major strategic mistakes. The U.S. seeks a new empire or sole leadership, particularly as it pertains to the Middle East. The U.S. has undertaken numerous unilateral actions. If the United Nations is favorable to the U.S., then the U.S. uses that to their advantage. If the United Nations disagrees with U.S. policies, then the U.S. takes unilateral actions. No one, no single center can today command the world. No single group of countries can do it. The world needs to be a multi-polar world without the perceived dominance of the United States.

When I digest the information above, the Middle East dominates my thinking. If I were to describe U.S. policy in the Middle East in one sentence, it would be this: "The U.S. is trying to hurry history." We are trying to create human rights progress with **coercive democracy**. Things need to happen on their own timing. Our government doesn't understand other countries' unwillingness to change according to our timing. If you judge historical U.S. human rights practices by today's standards, we were not much better than some of the countries we deplore today. We owned and mistreated slaves, we massacred Indians, we purposely killed civilians in Vietnam. If during the 1800s, a foreign country had pointed out our human rights violations and offered to help us improve in that area, we would have blasted them and told them to mind their own business. The author of the article on the previous page is Mikhail Gorbachev. *Does that change your thinking any? It shouldn'*t.

Let 's create a hypothetical country to give us an added perspective. This hypothetical country is decades ahead of us sociologically, economically, culturally, and militarily. This country is somewhat self-righteous and thinks that their way of doing everything is best. Their government wants to change our government to make it function more like theirs. This approach would make us angry and we would tell them to back off. Sometimes, I think the U.S. is this hypothetical country. Each country has to progress on human rights at its own speed. These other countries might well be headed in the right direction but are decades behind us in their maturation process. We are trying to hurry them along so that they can rise to our standards as quickly as possible. *This push to move other countries along the human rights scale is damaging our relationships with these other countries. We need to pull back on our campaign to advance human rights on our timing and standards, and quit jamming it down their throats.* Human rights never change quickly. They are a pillar in a society's makeup. Our contribution to other countries needs to incorporate greater assistance and less indoctrination.

The attitude the U.S. demonstrates around the world has caused us to be perceived as an arrogant country.

I have a friend who grew up in America but has spent the past thirty-three years living overseas. He travels extensively and attends international conferences several times annually. He knows several IOC (International Olympic Committee) members on a personal basis. He recently filled me in on the IOC selection process where Chicago was snubbed in favor of Rio de Janeiro. He told me that the anti-America sentiment is so strong around the world that unless we change our attitude, we might never host an Olympic Games again. Because of his insider information, my friend was able to explain to me why President Obama won the Nobel Peace Prize. He said that the rest of the world finally has hope that the U.S. will change its ways. The Nobel Peace Prize was merely a vote for Obama's expressed willingness to change our attitude. When the U.S. negotiates in ways that always favor us reminds me of the father who plays board games with his young son and always wins. The father gets the satisfaction of winning; but at the same time, he destroys his relationship with his son.

Presidents Kennedy and Reagan were very tough negotiators with the Soviet Union and succeeded. Because this tactic worked so well with the Soviet Union in the 1960s and 1980s, many people look at our victory over the Soviet Union and think Kennedy's and Reagan's tactics should always be our first line of offense and defense.

People are critical if we don't work every negotiation to our advantage. The way we now treat other countries has earned the U.S. the reputation of being a high-pressure salesman at best and a bully at worst. We always negotiate from a position of strength. In other words, we remind the other country, either directly or indirectly, that we have a strong military and that we use it if necessary. This tactic dooms the negotiating process from the start. The U.S. creates a "my way or the highway" method of negotiating with countries we don't like. When we tell these other countries that we will invoke sanctions or take military action if they refuse to adopt our way of thinking, we have poisoned the negotiating atmosphere. What do you think would happen if we humbled our- selves a bit as a means of negotiating? Let our enemies take the lead and have us respond to them instead of the other way around. All we have ever done is to negotiate in a way that drives the wedge between us deeper.

When our government representatives speak, I try to listen as if I was from another country. The way we negotiate with other countries is terrible. Our stated goal is to negotiate from strength. That's just being a bully. It's great to have strength, but you shouldn't promote it as a bargaining tool. I hear TV analysts discuss how they think we don't get enough concessions during our negotiations. These TV analysts think that we should always receive more in concessions than we give. Whatever happened to meeting in the middle? We have a mindset that we are supposed to win at negotiations. Negotiations are supposed to be where both sides win. It should be a win-win situation. The way we negotiate results in win-lose or more often lose-lose situations. This is just one more form of competitiveness that permeates our country. I honestly think that if we do a better job of making conciliations with our enemies, it will go further toward our national security (in the long run) than all the military weapons we can accumulate.

Making oneself vulnerable is a key element to making a relationship work, both personally and as a country. If you talk to relationship experts, you will learn that making oneself vulnerable is a prerequisite for creating a trusting relationship. The U.S. has been unwilling to make itself vulnerable to other countries and a self- fulfilling prophecy has emerged. We expressly negotiate from strength. This causes the other negotiating party(s) to become angry. We use that expressed anger to justify maintaining immense strength. Thus, the self-fulfilling prophecy has been created.

Our relationships with other countries have become very tenuous and sometimes awkward. Our unwillingness to make ourselves vulnerable creates a distinct barrier to having a workable, valid, meaningful, and trusting relationship with other countries or groups.

The problem with becoming more cooperative with our enemies at this stage is that it will put us at risk in the short run. Other countries might see our newfound conciliation as disingenuous. If that occurs, we could be victimized by our enemies. While we are pulling back from our decades-long uncompromising tactics, we will be at risk because other countries are not going to take us at face value. Why would they? Becoming more conciliatory and humble in our negotiations will not create an immediate fix because the trust is not there on either side; but over time, things should improve once the trust is recaptured.

Negotiating from strength is a self-fulfilling prophecy. Because we are not willing to make ourselves vulnerable, we create untenable relationships with other countries. Because we create these untenable relationships, we have to maintain and demonstrate our strength to keep these other countries at bay. If you have strength and power, you are going to need strength and power going forward. Flaunting your power makes other countries despise you; therefore, you need strength and power because you have strength and power. It is a self-fulfilling prophecy.

The U.S. has gone on record many times stating that we do not negotiate with terrorists or countries like Iran or North Korea. I can't understand why we do this. It costs nothing to find out what the other party's thinking is. Negotiating with other nations, sects, factions, or groups simply indicates our willingness to talk and listen with an open mind. Who knows? We might glean some valuable information during the talks that we have been unsuccessful in obtaining through normal intelligence methods.

When Iranian leader Mahmoud Ahmadinejad says he doesn't believe in the Holocaust, it's just his way of "pulling our chain." It seems that his strategy works pretty well. Libya has recently aggravated us without any intent to do so.

I watched the mastermind of the PanAm 103 bombing being repatriated to his home country of Libya. The citizens of Libya celebrated like it was New Year's Eve. Most Americans were incensed at the proceedings for two reasons. First, they were upset at Scotland for freeing a person that had caused so many deaths. Secondly, they were upset that the Libyan people were whooping it up upon his arrival back in his native country. The reason the bomber was released from prison is because he had terminal cancer and had at most six months to live. It was an act of compassion that caused Scotland to allow this man to return to his home country. Only a minority of Americans can appreciate this line of reasoning. Americans who got riled up because the Libyans celebrated this criminal's repatriation need to look at things from another perspective. Libya has virtually nothing to get excited about. They don't have professional sports. They don't go to movies. They live in one of the hottest places on Earth. They have virtually no true heroes. Their lives are mundane. The excitement the Libyan people exuded was not meant to insult any- body. If you lived as the Libyan people do, you might get really excited about welcoming home a repatriated countryman. What the Libyan people did was not meant to send a message to anyone. It was just a rare chance to cheer for something.

The world has always looked at the U.S. to provide

leadership. That is not true anymore. We have been such hypocrites; been caught in so many lies; and make up the rules as we go; that few counties want to follow our lead. Chinese students once protested in Tiananmen Square and some were killed by soldiers. The United States was quick to condemn China for its use of soldiers to kill student protesters. The Chinese were quick to shoot back, "What about Kent State?" On another occasion, there was a large power outage in the Northeast U.S. and Southeast Canada. One of our government representatives was quick to cite Canada as the culprit. A couple of days later after all the information had been analyzed, it was determined that the U.S. was at fault. The U.S. faults other countries for rounding up and massacring innocent citizens. That kind of stance makes us look bad when other countries bring up the My Lai massacre committed by U.S. troops on South Vietnamese citizens. These are just a few examples of U.S. hypocrisy that have served to spoil our relationships with other countries. The only difference in human rights violations perpetrated by other countries today and the ones perpetrated by the U.S. in the 1800s is time. We have progressed on our human rights at a faster pace than most countries. Because our human rights progression is ahead of these other countries, we push them to speed up. We want these other countries to advance according to our time- table. In the 1800s, we would never have accepted any other countries' offers to speed up our human rights timetable. The countries we are trying to push are likely to be as unreceptive of our influence as we would have been in the 1800s. Everybody has to progress on their own timing. It's unfortunate, but that's the way it works.

Death and Dying

As I get to know more about various cultures, I realize that most of what you think is "right" or "wrong" is merely a function of how you were raised. How do you feel about men taking their hats off when they are indoors? The way you feel is most likely a function of your family values or cultural belief system. Okay, now I'm in with one foot. Here comes the other. How people feel about death and dying is extremely personal and nobody should attempt to tell anyone else how to feel. I am tolerant of people whose practices involving death and dying are vastly different than my own. However, some common sense should be applicable to all situations, even death. I cannot understand spending millions of dollars digging up someone who died in a landslide or a mining cave-in just for the purpose of reburying them. I am not talking about money spent trying to rescue these people while there was a chance they were alive. I'm only talking about the money spent recovering the body far after death was an absolute certainty.

I also have a hard time with spending millions of dollars trying to recover the remains of people who died decades ago. We continue to spend enormous sums searching for the remains of WWII and Viet Nam soldiers. When I hear the families say that there is no amount of money too great to spend on recovering the remains of their loved ones, it just makes me realize that common sense is not part of the equation. Personally, I am for spending money on the living, not the dead.

How do you feel about this one? Often times more money is spent on a dying person during the last few months of his life than what he earned during his entire lifetime. It seems outrageous to spend that kind of money on someone who is destined to die in short order. I know —you all think I'm cold-blooded. I recall a situation where a person received $500,000 worth of hospital care during his last weeks on earth. I can think of numerous ways to spend that kind of money in a more productive manner. Spending $500,000 on college tuition for financially challenged students, or for scientific research, or for low income housing makes a lot more sense to me. I know people who are extremely stingy on giving to the living, but willingly shell out big bucks on the dead. That doesn't make sense. It reminds me of people who treat their pets better than they treat people.

Here comes a tuffie. How about pulling the plug on somebody? Most of my family members have made it clear that they want the plug pulled as soon as their chances for recovery are near zero. There are people who would make the case that people have made full recoveries from these dire situations. I question the validity of keeping millions of people on life support so that one person can become the "miracle statistic." It makes about as much sense as letting all the guilty prisoners go free to make certain that we don't accidentally have one innocent person in jail. Letting all the guilty people go free is nuts. I feel the same way about spending billions of dollars keeping millions of people on life support so that an occasional miracle can occur.

You can't put a price on a human life. Now what does that mean? It could mean that all people do not place the same value on human life. It could also mean that all human beings have the same worth. Is Adolph Hitler's life equal to Mother Teresa's? It seems that some people think you can't put a price on a human life because life is so precious that no amount of money is too great to spend on someone who is close to dying. There has to be a limit. You can't say there is no limit on human life just because there is no established criteria to do so. The idea that we should spend enormous sums on people because we can't put a finite price on a human life is ridiculous. I am ready for those of you who want to argue that I would feel differently if it were my loved one or me in that situation. I've thought this one through enough to know that I would not feel differently if it were one of my family members or me hanging in the balance. You would think that some people are destined to live forever (in this world) based on their philosophy for spending money on people at the very end of their lives.

Too Smart for Our Own Good

Sometimes people overanalyze problems. They believe problems to be more complex than they are. As a society, we might well be getting too smart for our own good. While technology has moved forward with leaps and bounds, human nature has remained virtually unchanged over time. Each generation repeats the mistakes of the previous generations. We think we are smart because we have so many new inventions. The reality is that while we create some great intelligence as a society, individually, we are not as smart as we think we are. Suppose a great war or some plague was to overcome the earth and only ten thousand people survived, all of them ordinary Americans. I am not convinced that those ten thousand people could not get us back to where we are today any faster than the first ten thousand people did.

There have been advances in our society that are easily identifiable as "opening Pandora's box" types of things: nuclear weapons, cloning, cosmetic surgery, and genetic engineering, just to name a few. While there are many positive sides to these advances, there are also potential pitfalls. Cloning is troublesome to me. I'm not sure what the ultimate goal is. It seems that things could get out of control. Who is supposed to make all the decisions?

There was a time when we had no computers, no cell phones, no copy machines, no microwave ovens, and no TV 's. I would like to make a case that these inventions have nothing to do with our happiness. The more things we own, the more things there are to manage and the more potential there is for something to go wrong. If we experience a week where the washing machine, the car, and the toilet all go haywire, we will have a nerve-racking week, regardless of what else happens. As we create new inventions and make advancements in technology, we are changing the relativity factor in a way that works against us. Time will tell if future advancements will make us happier or more miserable.

I don't think that I'll get too many arguments that things are not always what they seem to be. Commercials are my worst complaint. The commercials only tell you what they want you to know and distort the truth immensely. When a commercial says that a product is 20 percent better, what are they really saying? Is the product 20 percent better than the worst product on the market? Is the product 20 percent better than their previous product? Is the product 20 percent better than the best product on the market? You can't tell. There is no relativity. You must have something to compare 20 percent with to make the statement meaningful. Some companies will boast that they have attracted three hundred thousand new customers. What they should be required to tell you is that they also lost four hundred thousand customers, creating a net loss of a hundred thousand customers. All you hear about is the three hundred thousand customers gained. I wish they would make commercials tell the whole truth, not just the stuff they want you to hear.

When I watch TV commercials, I try to look beyond the obvious and see what else the commercial is saying. I saw a commercial that showed four guys in a car, and each one was using a different function on his cell phone. What I got out of this commercial is that four American adults would rather be engaged with their cell phones than to talk to each other. This is a sad commentary about our society.

Car commercials broadcast on the radio are probably the worst offenders about not telling the whole truth. At the tail end of their commercials, the salesmen ramp up their speech to the speed of an auctioneer so that nobody can understand what they are saying. What is it these salesmen are saying but don't want you to know?

These half-truths go beyond the business world. Try this statement on for size: Eighty percent of all car accidents occur within forty miles from home. This is a worthless statement. What are you supposed to do with this information? Are you supposed to start driving farther from home to be safer? The fact that eighty per- cent of all accidents happen within forty miles of home becomes meaningful only if a second relevant factor is introduced. If ninety percent of all miles are driven within forty miles of home and eighty percent of all accidents occur within forty miles of home, this means that driving within forty miles of home is safer than driving outside of forty miles. (The numbers I have supplied are hypothetical and are only used to make my point).

Politics is another arena in which things are not always as they seem. The way we pass laws in Washington always make a politician vulnerable to criticism. When bills are put to a vote, congressmen are sometimes voting on a conglomeration of interests provided by numerous senators and representatives (and lobbyists). Let's sup- pose that you are a U.S. senator. A bill comes up for a vote that has some really outstanding contents regarding taxation, education, and health care. Unfortunately, there is also a component that deals with storing nuclear waste in your state. You know the people of your state are dead set against storing nuclear waste in their back- yard. Consequently, you vote against the bill to pacify your constituents on the nuclear waste matter. What happens the next time you run for office? Your opponent will state that you voted against lowering taxes, improving education, and reforming health care. Your opponent would be correct, but it doesn't tell the whole story. This kind of stuff goes on all the time. I think a solution to this problem is that each item on a bill should be voted on independently. This would give each congress- man the ability to vote exactly how he or she feels about each issue. It would also help to eliminate "pork" from the bills. Another example where the truth is not as it seems is the issue of the Martin Luther King holiday (now Civil Rights Day). Arizona was the last state in the country to enact a holiday for Martin Luther King. They voted it down a couple of times before they finally passed it. The reason the proposition didn't pass the first two times is not because a majority of the voters were racist. The initiatives on the ballot were not conceived correctly and left the voters with a dilemma. Suppose you were a citizen of Arizona and had the following two propositions on the ballot to enact a holiday for Martin Luther King. (1) Do you want to raise taxes to establish a holiday for Martin Luther King, yes or no? (2) Which cur- rent holiday do you want to abolish in order to establish a holiday for Martin Luther King, Labor Day, Memorial Day, or Veteran's Day? You say you don't want to vote for either proposition. Congratulations. You are now a racist. The voters were finally presented with a proposition they could vote for, and the measure was passed. In the mean time, the state lost millions of dollars because of its tarnished reputation. The normally robust tour- ism trade suffered as a number of winter conferences were cancelled and moved to other states. Phoenix was stripped of hosting Super Bowl XXVII in order to pacify ardent activists wanting to penalize Arizona for their racist actions. Losing the Super Bowl was a huge blow to the economy.

PUTTING IT ALL TOGETHER

I have made my best effort to present you with some alternative ways to view our country. At times, I was very hard on our culture and societal norms. If you will recall, I presented the results of two studies that were trying to identify where the happiest people on Earth lived. One study concluded that the happiest people on Earth live in the rain forests of South America. The other study concluded that the happiest people on Earth lived in Costa Rica. The U.S. was far down the list on both studies, being ranked 114th in the world on the latter study. What these studies tell me is that gadgets, winning competitions, being a powerful country, and having enormous freedoms are not sources of genuine happiness. If our society truly wants to become happier, we need to make some fundamental changes.

There is one common denominator to everything I spoke about in this book. That common denominator is people. People create their happiness, and they create their unhappiness to a large degree. When I compare human nature in ancient Rome with our contemporary society, I see very little difference. We have come a long ways technologically, but human nature is unchanged through thousands of years. We have the same frailties and emotions as people from centuries gone by. We have the same need for greed and power. The methods we use to satisfy these needs have changed, but the principles remain the same. The Roman spectators flocked to their stadiums to watch Christians, lions, gladiators, and chariot racing. We flock to stadiums and arenas to watch "rage in the cage," ultimate fighting, football, boxing, wrestling, hockey, demolition derbies, and auto races. The Romans had wild sex parties. We have the sexual revolution. The Romans revered their military. We revere our military. When you compare the Roman Empire with our society, we demonstrate the same needs and frailties as the Romans but express them in different ways. The methods of expressing our needs have changed over time, but basic human nature has remained unchanged. Human nature is homogenous throughout the world and throughout time. If you need more convincing that human nature has not changed over time, I have something for you to think about. We have grown men who put on helmets and spend hours knocking each other down. After they get knocked down, these men get up and go knock somebody else down. Men get in a cage and try to tear each other apart. If there isn't a lot of blood spilled, the crowd boos. How far removed is this from the gladiators? Do you really think we've made progress psychologically and emotionally since the days of the Roman Empire?

Two things that could turn this country around the quickest are things that would require people to abandon some of their rights and freedoms. Our youth are the ones who can turn things around because they are still pliable and impressionable. I want to present two changes that, if adopted, would have a huge effect on changing our society around. The first change I would implement is to require all students to attend six weeks of boot camp the summer after their ninth grade. The second change I would like to implement is to require all students to live in Asia or Africa for two months during the summer after their eleventh grade. These two experiences would have a profound effect on our youth. They would become more respectful, disciplined, grateful, and self-confident. Even if a vast majority of people recognize that these programs would be great instruments in turning our country around, we still wouldn't be able to implement them because too many people value "my rights" over "our rights." The problem itself precludes a solution to the problem. We have to redefine freedom in ways that work for everybody, not just individuals. If we were fortunate enough to rally people behind these pro- grams, how would we pay for all of our youth to attend boot camp and live overseas for two months? Our prisons will start to empty out as more teenagers go through this attitude adjustment. We can use that savings to pay for these programs. The crime rate should go down. We can use this savings to pay for these programs. Less money should be needed by social programs because our youth will become stronger physically and mentally; they will be more self-confident; and they will become more reliable. The money spent on the youth of America should be viewed as an investment, not as an expense.

A third change I would like to implement is to overhaul our educational system in some drastic ways. I want to reduce the pressure that our children feel, do away with social graduation, and teach more life skills in high school.

The American public's outpouring of compassion during times of strife is truly amazing. It seems strange that people hardly know their neighbors, yet they all come together in times of need. Before the last century, the world was an incredibly tough place (physically) to live. People lived in constant times of need. People absolutely needed each other to survive. It was nearly impossible to be an island in those days. Today, we have islands everywhere.

Americans are quick to make judgments about people who commit moral or legal infractions; however, they are equally quick to forgive people who are willing admit to wrongdoings and demonstrate legitimate remorse. President Clinton missed a golden opportunity to take advantage of this trait of the American people. If he would have acknowledged his misconduct when he was first accused, demonstrated legitimate remorse, and asked for forgiveness, the whole incident would have blown over in short order. What created the furor was not his immorality but the ways he handled the situation after it became public.

We have had an on-going experiment in redefining freedom. I think many of us have made the realization that we can have only so much freedom before it begins to work against us. Unbridled freedom might work well for some individuals but is a menace for society as a whole. How do we rein in the excess freedoms that we have created? This will be a nearly impossible task and it will take generations to evolve and resolve.

If I can leave you with only one thought from this book, it is this. *Happiness and your outlook on life are functions of relativity and intent.* Let me remind you of how the *relativity factor* works. If I tell you that your next meal at a particular restaurant will leave you with a 95 percent chance of surviving, you would never eat at that restaurant again. If I told you that you had a 95 percent chance of surviving a parachute jump out of a burning airplane, you would be overjoyed with your chances. When you set a goal of producing one hundred units but produce only ninety units, you feel like a failure. If you set your goal at eighty units and produce ninety units, you feel great. Either way, you produced ninety units, but how you feel about producing ninety units is totally different. Here is another example of the *relativity factor.* A major league baseball player signs a contract making him the highest paid player in baseball. He feels great. Along come a couple of players who sign even bigger contracts. All of a sudden, the first player's happiness is not the same. The relativity factor has jumped up and bit him. Sometimes, I try to picture a world where everybody is happy. It can't happen. Based on the *relativity factor*, there will always be lots of unhappy people, even if everybody is doing well. People's happiness is not based on what they have accomplished or accumulated; it is based on how their accomplishments stack up in comparison to other people. Somebody is always in last place regardless of how well everybody is doing. What is good enough one day is not good enough the next; the bar has been raised. The relativity factor changes everything to our disadvantage.

The second thing I want you to take with you is a full understanding of intent. A person's intent should be the measuring stick for right and wrong. The outcome of a person's actions is not what counts. It 's their intent that counts. Please allow intent to be your guide in all that you do.

In order to become genuinely happy, both as individuals and as a country, we need to make some adjustments. We need to modify the ways we practice freedom. We need to change our outlook on work and money. We need to elect politicians who are elected for what they can do for their office, not what their office can do for them. They need to have the requisite insight to make good decisions and demonstrate a true sense of serving others. What it all comes down to is this: Are we willing to set lower goals to allow the relativity factor to work in our favor? The drawback to lowering your goals is that you will actually achieve less.

Which is a better deal: to achieve at a high level but be dissatisfied because you fall short of your established goal (sometimes perfection), or to be happy because you worked the relativity factor in your favor by setting and achieving lower goals?

The U.S. is undergoing a huge social upheaval. We have become a giant melting pot that is touted as being a great asset but ultimately may define our demise. When a country tries to honor and appease all religions, races, social misfits, cultures, special interest groups, and over- reactors, the country becomes dysfunctional. Our country is dysfunctional based on our concepts of freedom and equality. It is not possible to be all things to all people.

I want to leave you with a few examples that define our country. Abraham Lincoln could not get elected today. He was very homely-looking and lacked charisma. Mary Todd Lincoln was a borderline schizophrenic, which would be thoroughly exploited in today's politics. What does this say about our society? A second thing I want to convey deals with our freedoms. It is perfectly legal in the United States to operate a school to teach criminals how to become better criminals. This school could offer courses in guns, bank robbery, identification theft, how to operate a black market, and street fighting. Manufacturers of AK-47's, caskets, prison accessories, and brass knuckles could be key financial contributors to the school. Students could go online to obtain scholarships and grants from the government. This school might even throw in a GED program as an added incentive.

I hope you are sitting down as you read the following statements. Adolf Hitler admired America in the 1920s and 1930s because whites in America had demonstrated Aryan traits by asserting superiority over blacks, Indians, and some groups of immigrants. The KKK had even been allowed to flourish. Hitler even thought that America might be a good partner in seeking world dominance. How does this make you feel about your country, both past and present?

Printed in the United States
by Baker & Taylor Publisher Services